T0277541

Cambridge Elements

Elements in Critical Heritage Studies
edited by
Kristian Kristiansen, *University of Gothenburg*
Michael Rowlands, *UCL*
Francis Nyamnjoh, *University of Cape Town*
Astrid Swenson, *Bath University*
Shu-Li Wang, *Academia Sinica*
Ola Wetterberg, *University of Gothenburg*

UNDERSTANDING ISLAM AT EUROPEAN MUSEUMS

Magnus Berg
University of Gothenburg

Klas Grinell
University of Gothenburg

CAMBRIDGE
UNIVERSITY PRESS

CAMBRIDGE
UNIVERSITY PRESS

University Printing House, Cambridge CB2 8BS, United Kingdom

One Liberty Plaza, 20th Floor, New York, NY 10006, USA

477 Williamstown Road, Port Melbourne, VIC 3207, Australia

314–321, 3rd Floor, Plot 3, Splendor Forum, Jasola District Centre, New Delhi – 110025, India

103 Penang Road, #05–06/07, Visioncrest Commercial, Singapore 238467

Cambridge University Press is part of the University of Cambridge.

It furthers the University's mission by disseminating knowledge in the pursuit of education, learning, and research at the highest international levels of excellence.

www.cambridge.org
Information on this title: www.cambridge.org/9781108744195
DOI: 10.1017/9781108881623

First published 2021

A catalogue record for this publication is available from the British Library.

ISBN 978-1-108-74419-5 Paperback
ISSN 2632-7074 (online)
ISSN 2632-7066 (print)

Understanding Islam at European Museums

Elements in Critical Heritage Studies

DOI: 10.1017/9781108881623
First published online: July 2021

Magnus Berg
University of Gothenburg

Klas Grinell
University of Gothenburg

Author for correspondence: Magnus Berg, magnus.berg@globalstudies.gu.se

Abstract: Since 1989, exhibitions of Islamic artefacts in European museums have been surrounded by a growing rhetoric of cultural tolerance, in response to the dissemination of images of Islam as misogynist, homophobic and violent. This has produced a new public context for exhibitions of Islam and has led to major recent investments in new galleries for Islamic artefacts, often with financial support from the Gulf and Saudi Arabia. This Element addresses contemporary framings of Islam in European museums, focusing on how museums in Germany and the UK with collections of Islamic heritage realise the International Council of Museums (ICOM) definition of museums as institutions in the service of society. The authors find that far too often the knowledge of Islamic cultural heritage is disconnected from contemporary developments in museum transformations, as well as from the geopolitical contexts to which they are a response.

Keywords: Islamic art, museums, Islam in Europe, Islamic heritage, exhibitions

ISBNs: 9781108744195 (PB), 9781108881623 (OC)
ISSNs: 2632-7074 (online), 2632-7066 (print)

Contents

1 Introduction

Migrants who came to Europe from, for example, Turkey, Morocco or Pakistan in the 1970s and 1980s were referred to as Turkish, Moroccan or Pakistani immigrants. Today they are often labelled as Muslims. A symbol of this shift is the Rushdie affair in 1989. Different groups of immigrants, who had not previously been considered as having much in common, were suddenly lumped together into a large homogenous group: Muslims. A hitherto vague foreign threat had finally been given a face. The opposite of Europe, of all that was modern and civilised, was Islam. In 1989 it seemed obvious just how different Muslims were. They burned books (or at least a few hundred of them did). Ayatollah Khomeini, who was publicly portrayed as a spokesperson for the entire Muslim world, proclaimed a death sentence for a successful post-modern writer, one of the leading proponents of the notion of fluid and hybrid identities. However, the belief that Islam was the antithesis of modern, secular, European identity was not based solely on the violent reaction of some Muslims to Salman Rushdie's novel *The Satanic Verses*. Nor was it based solely on the fact that Europe had recently received many newcomers with a Muslim cultural background who also identified as Muslims, and practised Islam. Islam has always been a preferred opposite of Europe.

Even if the long history of Islamophobia is relevant, it is also important to note that contemporary Islamophobia has a specific context that distinguishes it from the millennia-old European denigration of Islam. Over the past thirty years the debate around immigrant Muslims in Europe has seen a shift, from a focus on ethnicity and foreignness to a differentiation of immigrant Europeans based on their religious identities (Allievi 2005). This new harsher focus on the religious identities of migrants is the effect of a variety of changes in European sociopolitical material circumstances, and in discourse. It is related to a growing Muslim presence in Europe, just as much as it is related to post-industrial emotional capitalism and neoliberal structural transformations. European social conflicts and migration, as well as armed resistance in the Middle East, South Asia and elsewhere in the 1970s, were regularly framed in socialist language. The major issues included imperialism, capitalism and class. Religion was rarely seen as a contributing factor, and social scientists even regarded it as an old-fashioned phenomenon in decline (Berger 1969). This has since changed. Religion is back on the societal radar (Berger 1999). 'Islam' is a prominent mobilising signifier for Muslims and non-Muslims alike.

The complex societal transformations of the past decades alluded to here have also led to a renewed interest in museums' collections of Islamic cultural artefacts (Junod et al. 2012). It might seem like a trivial subject when compared to war, terrorism or discrimination. Still, this Element is about Islam in European museums. It might be that museums have an institutional role to play in the service of society and its developments – at least the museums themselves claim that they do.

All over the world there have been major recent investments in new museum galleries for Islamic artefacts, often with financial support from Saudi Arabian donors. For example, the Victoria and Albert Museum in London opened the new Jameel Gallery of Islamic Art in 2006 and the Ashmolean Museum in Oxford opened the Prince Sultan bin Abdul-Aziz Al-Saud Gallery of the Islamic Middle East in 2009. The Louvre in Paris opened galleries of Islamic art in 2012 (with the Alwaleed bin Talal Foundation acting as the principal donor), and the British Museum opened the Albukhary Foundation Gallery of the Islamic World in October 2018 (after the research reported here had been concluded). All of the benefactors just mentioned have Saudi origins, with the exception of Albukhary who is a Malaysian businessman. The Museum of Islamic Art in Berlin is working on a renovation that is planned to be completed around the opening of the refurbished Museum Island in 2025. As we will discuss, all of these museums claim that they can play a role in countering Islamophobia and fostering cultural dialogue and understanding.

Islam in the museum world is found mainly in large Western museums of the more or less universal kind, where it is presented as one of a series of civilisations or world cultures. Most often 'Islam' is identified as a medieval phenomenon that serves as a bridge between East-Mediterranean Antiquity and the European Renaissance. This framing of Islamic culture is still visible in the spatial place of exhibitions on Islam in museums such as the British Museum in London, the Ashmolean in Oxford and Berlin's Museum Island, as well as in the Louvre in Paris, the Illinois Institute of Art in Chicago and the Metropolitan Museum of Art and Brooklyn Museum in New York. Sometimes Islamic culture is presented as a world culture disconnected from historical developments, as in the Museum Fünf Kontinente in Munich, the Montreal Museum of Fine Arts and the Ethnographic Museum in Dahlem, Berlin.

As this list of museums with Islamic galleries demonstrates, the presentation of Islamic materials is most often found in old and large national museum institutions. Even if it is often said that museums since the 1970s 'have shifted their priorities from the presentation of authentic artefacts and established taxonomies to the production of experiences where design, the originality of the display and performance are central to exhibitions' (Naguib 2015: 64), this shift is much less visible in these museums often called 'encyclopedic' or 'universal' (Cuno 2011; Lundén 2016).

We are only a few paragraphs into this text and already we have shifted between the terms Islam, Muslim and Islamic. With the renewed public prominence of religion, 'Islam' is on the tip of everyone's tongue. One point of this Element is to show that people can refer to very different phenomena when they say 'Islam'. This might give the impression that people, histories, countries and political developments that have very little to do with each other are driven by a monolithic force – Islam. In the seminal three-volume work *The Venture of Islam*, world historian Marshall Hodgson introduced the term Islamicate together with the term Islamdom as terminology that could differentiate religion from society and culture. Hodgson started by making a distinction between Islamic as a term for religious phenomena and Muslim as one for cultural traits common among Muslims. In order to discuss ideas and areas influenced by the Islamic religion, he coined the term Islamdom. Analogous to Christendom, Islamdom concerns the parts of society that deal with culture/civilisation. Hodgson urges us to talk about 'the society of Islamdom and its Islamicate cultural traditions'. The term Islamicate thus entails culture which has been shaped by Islamdom (countries and societies influenced by Islam). This should leave Islamic as a term for the religious aspects of these cultural traditions; like the term Christian art, so Islamic art would thus only pertain to artistic expressions of religious ideas and functions (Hodgson 1974: 31–58). Many writers within the field of Islamic art acknowledge that this really is a misnomer. If Hodgson's terminology had gained currency, the label would be Islamicate art instead of Islamic art (Blair & Bloom 2003). The label Islamicate is fitting when we want to include artefacts produced by Christians and Jews living within the lands of Islamdom. But the distinction between culture and religion attempted by the terminology has been shown to be impossible to uphold. Therefore we follow Shahab Ahmed's suggestion that '*all* acts and statements of meaning-making for the Self by Muslims and non-Muslims that are carried out in terms of Islam ... should properly be understood as *Islamic*' (Ahmed 2016: 544).

At the same time, it is important to stress that we are not looking to produce a definition of what 'Islam' is. We have studied what a handful of museums have chosen to label as Islam. Throughout our text, the term 'Islam' could be put in quotation marks. On only a few occasions have we actually searched for artefacts that could be called Islamicate. For practical purposes we try to use the word Islam according to the commonly understood and general meaning employed by the Oxford English Dictionary (OED) as 'The religious system established through the prophet Muhammad; the Muslim religion; the body of Muslims, the Muslim world'. Even if we were to try to describe how the individual exhibitions understand Islam, we would also be assuming that most visitors hold the general understanding that Islam is the name of one of our world religions.

But what is a religion, then? Within religious studies there are a number of competing definitions that most often attempt to challenge the perceived Protestant bias which equates religion with an organised and scripture-based belief in God. Many in religious studies hold that a common definition of everything that even the different world religions encompass cannot be found. Others, such as Graham Harvey in his book *Food, Sex and Strangers: Understanding Religion as Everyday Life*, argue that religion has as much to do with the sacrifice of goats as it does with the belief in God (Harvey 2013; Stausberg & Gardiner 2016). The OED states that the most common definition of the term religion is the 'Belief in or acknowledgement of some superhuman power or powers (esp. a god or gods) which is typically manifested in obedience, reverence, and worship; such a belief as part of a system defining a code of living, esp. as a means of achieving spiritual or material improvement'. Also, when it comes to 'religion', we see the merits of a critical and precise terminology, even if we sometimes utilise its laxer meanings.

Our investigations into the images of Islam are also very much related to another term which is both contested and vague: Islamophobia. It has often been criticised on the grounds that being critical of or against Islam has nothing to do with having a phobia. Still, the term has a strong following and does not need to be read as literally meaning phobia, but rather as a term which covers a distinct anti-Muslim racism. The most widely used definition of the term comes from the British Runnymede Trust which states that:

> Islamophobia is any distinction, exclusion, or restriction towards, or prefer-
> ence against, Muslims (or those perceived to be Muslims) that has the
> purpose or effect of nullifying or impairing the recognition, enjoyment or
> exercise, on an equal footing, of human rights and fundamental freedoms in
> the political, economic, social, cultural or any other field of public life.
>
> (Runnymede Trust)

The Runnymede Trust stresses that this is not only an analytical definition; it is also aimed to point to recommendations on how to respond to it. As we shall see, the definition thus directly involves the museums who explicitly want to be part of this response. It is not a term we will use, and our discussion does not really involve any examples of Islamophobia. In our material we rather find a sort of misdirected and back-firing Islamophilia.

Even if there are a good deal of shared developments happening simultaneously in the USA and Europe, there are also important differences between these two contexts. In Europe, heritage management has until very recently had a national frame, while in the USA it has been more multi-levelled from the outset (Harrison 2013: 20). The contemporary sociopolitical contexts also have important differences, making it relevant to focus on Europe here. Even if prejudice and animosity towards Islam are widespread and pronounced both in the USA and Europe, the everyday interactions affected by this discourse are quite different. This is due to differing histories of colonial domination, migration and the deep historical presence of Islam in many parts of Europe, among other things.

Some of the most vocal proponents of European intolerance today are populist nationalists who portray Islam as the single greatest threat to European values and culture. They claim that there is a fundamental incompatibility between European and Islamic values. Many studies have been done on the contemporary rise of Islamophobia and prejudiced representations of Islam. However, these studies demonstrate a systematic neglect of perspectives based on heritage and representations of Islam at museums (Allen 2010; Deltombe 2005; Fekete 2009; Yaqin & Morey 2011; Green 2015; Kundnani 2015). Pre-Covid-19, European museums had over 500 million visitors annually (EGMUS – The European Group on Museum Statistics), and museums have been central institutions to the formation of European national identities (Bennett 1995; Moore & Whelan 2007). A number of recent projects have investigated how museums still play an important role in the formation of European and national identities (Aronsson 2011; Kaiser, Krankenhagen & Poehls 2012; Peressut et al. 2013).

The museums in Europe with large collections of Islamic artefacts have hardly been researched within critical museology or heritage studies. These collections have been the domain of the almost autonomous field of Islamic art; that is, a field that is still self-enclosed and object centred, dominated by cultural history and the analysis of specific artefacts (Blair & Bloom 2003; Flood 2007; Junod et al. 2012; Necipoğlu 2013). This can make Islam seem like an exceptional case and can thus disconnect the knowledge on Islamic cultural heritage from contemporary questions of identity and political framing (Knell et al. 2012: 38). As Beshara Doumani says, 'redefining the concept of Islamic art in the museum context is ultimately about reconfiguring Europe's vision of itself and its relation to the Other' (2012: 129).

In the more socially and theoretically engaged research on museums there is a vast array of works on how exhibitions are affected by political and social conditions (Vergo 1989; Karp & Levine 1991; Hooper-Greenhill 1992; Bennett 1995; McDonald 1998; Coombes & Phillips 2015), as well as advice on how museums should counter prejudice and promote integration (Sandell 2007;

Golding 2009; Lynch & Alberti 2010; Schorch 2013). Almost nothing of this literature concerns Islam or Muslims. Even the growing field of Studies of Religion in Museums gives surprisingly little attention to Islam (Paine 2013: 18–19, 32–33; Claussen 2010; Lüpken 2011; Minucciani 2013; Kamel 2013; Buggeln et al. 2017).

There are thus very few previous works with a sociopolitical perspective on Islam and museums (Shatanawi 2009, 2012a, 2012b; Kamel 2004, 2013, 2014; Norton-Wright 2020). In the UK there is good documentation on the re-imaginings of the gallery of Islamic art from the Victoria and Albert Museum and the British Museum (Moussouri & Fritsch 2004; Crill & Stanley 2006; Fakatseli & Sachs 2008), as well as a thesis in archaeology on the local representations of Islam in British museums with extensive data on displays and visitor surveys (Heath 2007).

The above-mentioned sociopolitical developments have meant that exhibitions of Islamic artefacts since 11 September 2001 have been framed as expressions of cultural tolerance, co-existing with both acts of terror and violence in Islam's name, and Islamophobic images of Islam as misogynist, homophobic and violent. This has produced a radically new frame for the exhibiting of Islamic artefacts which used to be directed at a select few connoisseurs (Grabar 2012). Within the heritage sector, cultural heritage is often said to be useful in promoting tolerance and global understanding (Report of the Working Group on Cross Cultural Issues of ICOM, 1997). But can the fear of a coming Eurabia be quelled into tolerance by using the Islamic cultural heritage from collections at European museums?

At least since World War II there has also been a broader frame for museum exhibitions. UNESCO (United Nations Educational, Scientific and Cultural Organization) and ICOM (International Council of Museums) were both founded following the end of the war, based on the belief that culture and heritage can foster international understanding and peace. The EU (European Union) later formulated policy declarations built on these postulates (Höglund 2012). At the 1972 ICOM assembly in Santiago de Chile, it was argued that museums should work harder to become 'an integral part of societies around them', and the definition of museum was complemented with the phrase that it should be 'an institution in the service of society and its development' (Report of the Working Group on Cross Cultural Issues of ICOM).

The current ICOM definition of museum reads:

> A museum is a non-profit, permanent institution in the service of society and its development, open to the public, which acquires, conserves, researches, communicates and exhibits the tangible and intangible

heritage of humanity and its environment for the purposes of education, study and enjoyment. (ICOM)

With the ICOM Cultural Diversity Charter of 2010 museums are called to stand for the 'recognition and affirmation of cultural diversity at the local, regional and international levels and the reflection of this diversity in all policies and programs of museums across the world' (ICOM Cultural Diversity Charter). This frames the way in which Islamic collections and galleries are presented, and it is also the frame for our analysis in this Element. We can see that museums have also adopted this frame:

> In the difficult climate currently surrounding the public discourse on Islam, the Museum für Islamische Kunst sees itself as a mediator of a culture of great sophistication. Its exhibitions uncover the history of other cultures, something which in turn helps foster a better understanding of the present. This lends the collection its sharp political relevance, both within Germany and abroad, as a cultural storehouse for Islamic societies and peoples.
>
> (Museum für Islamische Kunst, Berlin)

In a 2004 article in *The Guardian*, the former director of the British Museum, Neil MacGregor, argued that his museum could make important contributions also outside of the UK and Europe:

> The new interim government in Iraq will have to consider how it defines Iraq's identity. And it will be surprising if it does not turn, as every other government in the Middle East has turned, to historical precedents to define the wished-for future. There is nowhere better to survey those precedents than the British Museum. (MacGregor 2004)

The hopes that MacGregor expressed for recognition and understanding were striking. Their fulfilment has to do with a certain kind of temporal connection. It is believed that by looking back through history and visually exploring the artefacts connected with an Islamic past, we will finally understand Islam's place in the current political situation. We journey from the present to the past and then back to the present, equipped with new historical knowledge that makes the present more readily understandable. Those who undertake this journey have been given the keys needed to unlock our current intolerant political situation. That is the frame. The problematic discourse on Islam can be counteracted, and the Muslim world can emerge as something other than a seat of conflict. A dialogue between cultures can be developed and fanaticism – both Muslim and European – can be resisted. Perhaps Iraq might even be able to find a new national identity. These are no small claims. In this Element we attempt to evaluate this 'frame of tolerance' by relating it to the (few) actual Islamic galleries at European museums that visitors encounter.

According to Gülru Necipoğlu, the recent past has seen an increase in stereotypes and outdated approaches to Islamic visual cultures, strengthened in part by documentaries, exhibitions and new museums of Islamic art. There is a gap between simplistic popularisations of Islamic cultural heritage and the growing complex academic interpretations of Islamic visual cultures (Necipoğlu 2013). The version of Islam presented in museums is framed as a separate civilisation of the past lacking any direct connection with Islam as experienced in today's Europe. This is also seen in the evaluation of the galleries of Islamic art at the Victoria and Albert Museum (Fakatseli & Sachs 2008). As we shall see in Section 2, this has a grounding in the existing collections of Islamic art and how they came to be. Later, the framing of Islamic art in European museums has been influenced by Traditionalism; an ideology that relies on a Romantic construction of mythical origins that frames Islam as an esoteric and traditional Wisdom, rather than as the faith of fellow European citizens. Taken together, this makes the European category of Islamic art ill prepared to fill the role assigned to it as a gateway to understanding living Muslims or Islam's role in contemporary Europe (Grinell 2018b, 2020).

Certain temporary exhibitions falling outside of the scope of our project have tried to portray Islam as a local lived aspect, but the large investments are still focused on Islamic art. Mirjam Shatanawi has argued that 'tolerant' exhibitions of Islamic collections might even reinforce 'the proposition of a contrast between contemporary Islam (stagnant and intolerant) and early Islam (advanced and tolerant), which informs much of global politics' (Shatanawi 2012a: 179).

This Element aims to give new critical contributions to both museology and the research on images of Islam in Europe. In order to do this, we might also need to use a less celebratory understanding of cultural heritage. The discrepancy that Necipoğlu saw and criticised between the scholarly and popular exposés of Islamic art might also be understood as the difference between history and heritage. David Lowenthal writes that 'collapsing the entire past into a single frame is one common heritage aim' and 'stressing the likeness of past and present is another' (1998: 139). Scholars in the field of Islamic art are engaged in historical research – they are trying to find answers to specific questions about localised materials. When history is used for contemporary political and identitarian purposes it transforms into heritage, to borrow Lowenthal's parlance. Heritage is something people do as they use history to understand, negotiate or market their identities (Lowenthal 1998; Harrison 2013).

European framings of Islamic heritage present it as a closed other, evoking the idea that the visitor should learn to respect the people and the traditions that were able to produce such masterpieces. As Shatanawi writes, 'the preferred strategy is to focus on universal love of aesthetics; substituting beauty for violence and artistic skill for backwardness' (Shatanawi 2012a: 177).

This Element is the result of the research project Museological Framings of Islam in Europe, funded by the Swedish Research Council. From 2015 to 2018 we visited museums mainly in the UK and Germany which advertised exhibits related to 'Islam'. We approached the exhibitions via framing theory.

A critical frame analysis starts by a 'mapping of the different ways in which an issue is framed' (Verloo & Lombardo 2007). Frames can have the form of mentalities, ideologies, structures, institutions, artefacts and behaviour, and function to organise experience and guide action (Goffman 1974; Snow 2011). In exhibition analysis we treat words, objects, design, architecture and all the minute details of an exhibition as frame elements that make the exhibited topic understandable (Bal 2015: 417). With inspiration from linguistic frame theory, we distinguish between invoked and evoked frames (Fillmore 2008; Petruck 2008).

We read this in relation to Judith Butler's argument that when a cultural phenomenon is not framed as an intelligible life, it will not be recognisable and will thus not gain social or political recognition. Lives that fall outside of the societal frames will not be guarded against injury and violence in the same manner as those inside the frame. Those that are framed as fundamentally other are thus not intelligible, and thereby not recognised as mutually precarious and injurable (Winter 2008; Butler 2009). Cultural, and museological, frames have social agency.

Our empirical analysis focuses on what framings of Islam are evoked by the exhibitions we have visited, in response to the above sociopolitical frame that we as visitors invoke (Grinell 2020). Our main question is if and how exhibitions of Islamic heritage evoke tolerant understandings of Islam, and thus fulfil the museums' service to society.

More concretely, our analysis has been guided by four basic questions:

What is Islam? Is Islam a religion, a culture, an aesthetical tradition or something else? If it is a religion, is it a belief, a set of rituals, commandments or something else?

Where is Islam? Is it limited to the traditional lands of the Middle East and North Africa? Are other Islamic countries represented? Is there any mention of countries outside the Muslim world where Islam is a minority religion?

When is Islam? Does Islam have a pre-history before the revelations of the Prophet Muhammad? At what point in time does the presentation of Islam end?

Who is Islam? Is Islam represented by any actors or individuals? What are their ethnicities, class, gender, etc.? What social constellations are these actors inscribed in?

As said, 'Islam' here is an open label filled out by the exhibitions we have studied. Our aim is to present what European museums have to say about 'Islam'.

2 Collecting

As already indicated, there is one particular form in which Islam is represented first and foremost in European museums: as Islamic art, or, in German, Islamische Kunst. Islamic art is usually found at larger museums – the kinds of museums that are well known and which appear on lists of places 'one should visit in one's lifetime' because of their size or reputation. One thing they have in common is also that they are old. In terms of museum-historical measurements, they are considered very or fairly old. There are four such museums that we have visited: the British Museum and Victoria and Albert Museum in London, Museum für Islamische Kunst at the Pergamon Museum in Berlin and the Ashmolean Museum of Art and Archaeology in Oxford. (One can discuss to what extent the latter museum lives up to the criteria of size and fame. But there is no reason to be fussy here.) Museum für Islamische Kunst, as evidenced by the name, is devoted entirely to Islamic art. The other three each contain separate galleries for Islamic art (the British Museum has now remade its galleries).

These exhibitions display objects. The objects are, almost always, taken from the museum's own collections, which contain many more things than those on display. The collections, therefore, offer the exhibition producers a great degree of freedom to decide what they want to display when they put together an exhibition. At the same time, since permanent exhibitions are meant to display the collection highlights, the collections frame the freedom of the museum (Svanberg 2015). The museums own many objects, but far from everything. 'The Islamic world' contains infinitely many more objects than the largest museum storage can accommodate. The collections, therefore, consist of a very specific selection of what has been possible and worthy for the museums to acquire and save. This selection has been made in accordance with specific principles and based on certain prerequisites. The principles deal, as we shall see, with what is considered to be worth collecting, classifying and storing (and possibly displaying). The prerequisites are primarily economic, political and logistical, and determine what is considered to be worth collecting.

This is the compelling background of the exhibitions: the collections and the principles and prerequisites that created them. In order to understand the exhibitions, one must understand the collections and their origin.

As mentioned before, these four museums are old. The Ashmolean Museum was established in 1683 (thus claiming to be the UK's oldest public museum) (Wodehouse 2014). The British Museum was founded in 1753, while the Victoria and Albert Museum was founded in 1852, as a direct consequence of the Great Exhibition of Works of Industry of All Nations in 1851, as the Museum of Manufactures, and shortly thereafter renamed South Kensington Museum (Victoria and Albert Museum). The Museum für Islamische Kunst was founded in 1904 as a department of the Kaiser-Friedrich Museum (later renamed the Bode Museum), and opened in the same year. In 1932 the museum became an independent part of the newly built Pergamon Museum (Wodehouse 2014). The largely museum-based academic study of Islamic art in Europe is younger than the first two museums, but roughly contemporary with the latter two.

In order to understand the origins of the exhibitions we visited, we must focus on the second half of the nineteenth century. At that time, according to Oleg Grabar, a principal researcher in the field of Islamic art and architecture, the European elite shared four 'experiences' that paved the way for academic and museum interests in Islamic art (Grabar 2012). The first was an 'Orientalist syndrome', 'whereby luxury and beauty were best expressed in objects made in the East and in styles based upon these objects or viewed as "Oriental"'. This view was part of the exotic, romanticising streak of the Orientalist discourse which Edward Said discussed in detail in his seminal book *Orientalism* (Said 1978). There it shared a place with its opposite: the demonising image of the Orient as dangerous, oppressive, violent and so on.

The second experience was the increased travel of Europeans in Muslim countries. In most cases, this was undertaken for professional reasons. The travellers were merchants, missionaries, mercenaries, specialised technicians, diplomats – and adventurers and explorers. Eventually, commercial tourism also followed.

The journeys aroused a curiosity for oriental forms and extended to the purchasing of souvenirs that could be made randomly – you bought anything that looked attractive in the Oriental bazaars – or fastidious. The latter was largely related to carpets and textiles.

Thirdly, which is one of the prerequisites of the other factors, the period was characterised by conquest and colonialism. In Said's analysis, these military conquests are symbiotic to a conquest of the Orient in terms of knowledge. The colonial powers regarded themselves as destined to gather knowledge of the

Orient and arranged this knowledge according to what Western thinking found to be best. This mission also served as justification for military conquest. Western culture reigned over the most advanced knowledge in the world and how it should evolve, and therefore it was the duty of Westerners to take political responsibility for the world.

Finally, the period saw the start of systematic gathering of Islamic artefacts. This was conducted primarily by private individuals who had economic resources and a passion for the matter. This entailed ceramics, glass, carpets and weapons. From the beginning, these collections were kept intact and in the private ownership of the collectors, but eventually a large portion of the objects moved into a more public world: to the art and antiques market and, through sale, deposit or as gifts, to the museums.

2.1 Inspiration

It is usually said that there were two main reasons why the museums were interested in Islamic art. One was related to handicraft and its future development; the other related to the history of art and culture. The first reason was thus primarily aimed towards the future, the other towards the past.

There are a number of museums that have their conceptual origins in the series of world exhibitions that began in 1851 in London with the Great Exhibition of the Works of Industry of All Nations. The ambition was that these would favour technical and industrial development through a peaceful competition among various nations.

The most prominent example of museums with this background is the museum which is now called the Victoria and Albert Museum. It opened in 1852 immediately after the World Exhibition as the Museum of Manufactures. In 1854, the name was changed to South Kensington Museum after the area it would move to and where it is currently located, and acquired its current name in 1899.

The Victoria and Albert Museum focuses on handicraft, on 'decorative arts' – the world's largest of its kind. Slightly simplified, one could say that fear was the main motivator behind artisan crafts being the focus for the museum and the exhibition. Most people believed that Britain was the world's most advanced nation when it came to the industrial manufacturing of consumer goods. But many felt that tasteful craftsmanship had taken the backseat to mass-produced items. New technology and new forms for production created things that were not beautiful enough. The beauty of the material world that surrounded people was threatened.

This was the claim of the Arts and Crafts Movement in Britain, with John Ruskin and William Morris as leading names. For this movement, criticism of the idiom of industrialism and an emphasis on craft-based aesthetics were fundamental. Popular craftsmanship and medieval design were examined in order to find inspiration and material for innovative thinking. But ideas suitable for the development of European design were also picked up from the Orient. Ideas came from Japan and China, but also from the world dominated by Muslims. On the whole, Islamic art played a very important role in European, and not least British, arts and architecture in the second half of the nineteenth century – even to the extent that John Sweetman called his book on this subject *The Oriental Obsession*: an obsession, or pure fixation, which culminated precisely at this time (Sweetman 1987).

Examples of good design encouraged craftsmen and industrialists to aesthetically think beyond the industrially framed forms. This was primarily why the Islamic objects found their place at the Victoria and Albert Museum, not as artefacts testifying to historical conditions in another part of the world. This is why no particular attention was initially paid to cataloguing facts about the objects that are currently considered important: the manufacturer's name, (as) exact (a) date (as possible) and the like (Stronge 2000). Today there is still a magnificent Persian carpet from the sixteenth-century Safavid dynasty exhibited at the museum which is known as 'The Chelsea Carpet'. It carries this name because not much was known about its history. However, the museum was aware that it was purchased from an antique dealer in Chelsea, London, about one kilometre to the south.

The museum started collecting carpets roughly twenty-five years after its opening. The reason for doing so had to do with the 'Schools of Design' that had been established in England. The school failed to achieve its goal: to improve the design of industrially produced textile products. The problem was, it was believed, that the students were taught to imitate the forms of nature as realistically as possible. This was a 'false principle' for design, because the three-dimensionality of nature contradicted the two-dimensional flatness of the textile. True principles, however, existed in medieval and oriental textile art. Therefore it was the task of South Kensington Museum to acquire oriental carpets. Again, it was the aesthetic form and not the cultural-historical context which was important.

Old carpets were of particular interest. Newer ones had been increasingly designed to meet the expectations of a growing European consumer group, and if the museum bought such carpets, it could accelerate this development. Old carpets were acquired from two locations, either from merchants and stores in London or via northern Europeans who had been sent to or who were already stationed in Islamic countries. The most prominent of the latter was Robert Murdoch Smith, the museum's agent in Persia (Wearden 2000). In 1873 he offered his services to the museum, after already having spent ten years in the country. He had worked as head of the Persian part of a project dedicated to constructing a telegraph line from Great Britain to India for the 'Indo-European Telegraph Department'. In competition (but also in collaboration) with purchasers from other European countries, he purchased carpets for the museum, as well as other objects – ceramics, metalwork, manuscripts. The European Persian antiquities market expanded gradually during Murdoch Smith's Persian period, and he and other Europeans took advantage of all the contacts and accessible paths they had in order to meet this demand. However, retailers sold others unaffiliated with museums. They were especially favoured by a long period of drought and famine in Persia, culminating in 1871–2, when perhaps as many as 2 million people died. This created a situation where, in order to survive, Persians were inclined to sell inherited articles and other possessions (Vernoit 2000).

2.2 A Tree

The second reason for the museums' interest in Islamic art thus had to do with the history of art and culture. This was a time when science was busy producing series and taxonomies. On the assumption that younger forms had developed from older ones, historical objects were classified in order to determine how they were connected in time. The perspective was highly evolutionistic. The elementary converted into the complex step by step, the rough into the refined and the inferior into the superior.

When contemporary scholars of Islamic art critically discuss this era, one particular image is referenced: Bannister Fletcher's pedagogical illustration 'Tree of Architecture' from *A History of Architecture on the Comparative Method for Students, Craftsmen and Amateurs* by father and son Bannister Fletcher, first published in 1896 (Fletcher & Fletcher 1896). The image aims to show how the historical architectural styles of the world are interrelated in their development. What appears then is a tree. Its trunk represents the continual, general development of all styles. There Greek, Roman and Romanesque (which include 800 to the 1200s in what is anachronistically known as Western Europe) styles are inscribed. Branches spread from the trunk, and at the top is, as expected, the crown. In the latter there is unbroken plant power in three layers: Gothic, Renaissance and, at the top, modern styles (which are inspired by the two previous ones). In the branches which extend from the trunk, into nothing and emptiness, there are styles from which no further development sprouted. They are branches that have stopped growing – blind alleys, to use another metaphor.

A certain pair of branches is of particular interest here. One branch extends to the left towards the Byzantine style and the other to the right towards the 'Saracenic'; that is, the Islamic. The trunk continues upward via the Romanesque style.

This placement of the 'Saracenic' style agrees well, Gülru Necipoğlu argues, with the orientalist image of the world that Said analysed (Necipoğlu 2012). The perspective is Eurocentric and marks a dividing line, or perhaps a crossroads, between East and West. Islamic art becomes an unchanging style, fixed in a medieval past. It lacks the power to develop new architectural directions, thereby distinguishing itself from European styles that have 'progressed by the successive solution of constructive problems' (Fletcher & Fletcher 1896: 604).

The four big museums with Islamic collections studied here are classifying systems in themselves. This applies to both the collections and the exhibitions. In addition, they can be called universal museums (something that, in any case, the British Museum explicitly calls itself): they attempt to reflect all the world's cultures and history, to the extent that is possible. The museums do not believe they have actually managed to capture this vastness, but they still strive to do their best. Museum für Islamische Kunst lacks universal ambitions, but it should be noted that it is part of the Pergamon Museum (as one of three museums), which in turn is one of the museums at the Museuminsel in Berlin. And the Museuminsel makes clear claims to universality.

We have already mentioned that it would be impossible to collect every kind of fragment from near and far. One must base choices on certain principles. But the collected articles must also be arranged in a way that creates a sense of both transparency and orderliness. Totalising schemes derived from academic research, such as the Tree of Architecture, offer such systematics. These can organise related objects, and indicate which object should be contained and excluded in specific departments. If this should be done in a way that makes universality easier to grasp, then the different departments must also be made comparable to one another. When modern museums began to emerge, a kind of systematics was already present. This entailed well-defined categories waiting to be filled with content. And the more categories that a museum could fill, the closer the museum had come to achieving universality.

At least as far as the British Museum is concerned, this was the logic behind the Islamic collections and thus also behind the exhibition of Islamic art. This was, above all, represented by someone who had a great impact on the emergence of the British Museum of today: Augustus Wollaston Franks (1826–97) (Wilson 1997; Ward 1997, Ward 2000). He has been called the second founding father of the museum (the first being Sir Hans Sloane (1660–1753)). From his appointment in 1851 as an assistant at the Department of Antiquities, through his time as a curator for the 'Mediaeval Antiquities and Ethnography' department formed in 1866, to his death in 1897, the museum underwent extensive changes with Franks as a driving force. The collections grew in volume, but also encompassed larger geographic areas. In fact, the collections covered almost all areas – it was during this time that the museum became universal at least in terms of geography. During the first half of the 1800s, the collections were completely dominated by the ancient world around the Mediterranean (and of natural history), and after Franks' death, they contained objects from nearly the entire world.

This was the result of Franks' systematic purchases to the museum. But in addition to these, Franks also had an extensive private collection. This was made possible by personal funds which also enabled him to – as one might expect from a gentleman – abstain from wages from the museum. He donated parts of his collections to the museum and he often persuaded his friends, who were also collectors, to do the same. This was one of Franks' talents: to form friendships with people in the Western world who shared his interests. Many of these friends were researchers rather than collectors. One of them was Dane Jens Jacob Worsaae, who once served as an assistant to Christian Jürgensen Thomsen. It was Thomsen who devised the separation of pre-history into Stone, Bronze and Iron Ages and Worsaae further refined this periodisation. Franks applied this system when he organised the museum's archaeological collections.

But classification was used on more than pre-history. It was Franks' view that the museum should function as a coherent scheme in which one could make comparisons between material products from as many of the world's cultures as possible. This meant that connections, influences and lines of development, as well as crossroads and dead ends, could be illustrated. Thus, it also became necessary to acquire the kinds of objects that made comparisons possible. For the Islamic collections, this had certain consequences. Carpets and textiles were not regarded as objects that worked particularly well in the museum's comparative systems. They were rather sent to the South Kensington Museum, which is an important explanation for why the Victoria and Albert Museum today has such a large collection of oriental carpets. The British Museum preferred to have objects made of glass, ceramics (in particular), metal and the like – all more suitable than textiles for cross-cultural comparisons.

The fact that certain objects from the Islamic world ended up at the British Museum was not the result of Franks' great passion for them. He was not uninterested, but he could hardly be called a committed authority in the field. His passion was for the comparative and evolutionary system itself. There was a box available for Islamic art which should be filled with forms that could be placed against other forms. The role of Islamic art in the system was to contribute to the understanding of art developed from classical Antiquity to the Renaissance.

By focusing on the forms and how they were connected, other aspects were pushed to the background. These aspects included the cultural, historical and religious contexts that the objects were previously grouped into, for example. It is likely that Franks lacked substantial knowledge about these aspects. For instance, Franks and his wealthy friends did not buy oriental objects from the Orient, but rather from art and antique dealers in Paris and London.

In Germany, the scientific interest in Islamic art took longer to flourish (Hagedorn 2000). In the middle of the nineteenth century more focus was placed on oriental languages and history than on art and architecture. When scholars started to write about Islamic art, it was not in a very appreciative way. Arab architecture was considered imperfect when it was placed next to European examples and some tried to explain this by attributing certain peculiarities to the Arab mentality. It was seen as excessive and nomadically unrestrained, and for a people viewed as fiery and impulsive, it was boring and cold to enter into the systematically coherent thinking that satisfactory artistic and architectural work required.

Another way of looking at the matter developed within the reform movement in the field of art handicrafts, in the United Kingdom referred to as Arts and Crafts, which reached Germany as well as other European countries. There, Islamic art was valued and seen as possessing a vital and energising power. Much was written from this perspective during the second half of the nineteenth century.

Eventually, attention to Islamic architecture began to change. It became more open, less governed by stereotypes, more inquisitive and appreciative. Certain aspects, in particular Ottoman, mosque architecture, were considered worth serious study. The academic circle that discussed Islamic art had begun to expand. This culminated in 1910 at an exhibition in Munich, entitled *Meisterwerke Muhammedanischer Kunst*, which paved the way for a greater understanding of Islamic expression. It was seen as a failure, to a certain degree as it did not pique the interest of a broader audience, and the reviewers described it as boring and joyless. But it was still deemed a success. It caught the attention of a number of modernist artists in Germany and elsewhere. For example, in letters and diaries Wassily Kandinsky, Franz Marc and Henri Matisse expressed their admiration for the exhibition and the exhibited objects.

But neither the artistic reform movement nor the Munich exhibition in 1910 was the most important event for the German study of Islamic art. Rather, it was a man born in Berlin in 1865 (Gonella 2015; Kröger 2015; Weber 2015). He is most important to our Museum für Islamische Kunst perspective, but also for Germany in general. This man was Friedrich Sarre. He, like Franks, was financially independent, at least until World War I (during which he, as a liberal-conservative supporter of the emperor, lost his inherited wealth through the purchase of war bonds). After mainly art history – but also military – studies he started working as an assistant at the royal museums in Berlin, which aroused his interest in Islamic artefacts.

Like Franks, Sarre was a private collector and surrounded by a circle of like-minded individuals. Many of his friends – bankers and other well-appointed people – were mainly attracted to the exoticism of the Orient and decorated their homes in an oriental style. Sarre was not entirely unaffected by this craze – there are photos where he and his children are dressed in oriental outfits – but his collecting was exclusively scientifically and museologically motivated. As with Franks, Sarre also donated parts of his collections to the museums he served. And, similar to Franks, he exhibited some of his pieces in what would become the Islamic department of the Kaiser-Friedrich Museum (which later became the Bode Museum after its founder, Wilhelm von Bode, with whom Sarre co-operated). In 1932, this museum would be transformed into the Museum für Islamische Kunst.

Franks and Sarre thus had a lot in common. But they were also different. Sarre specialised in Islamic art (although his knowledge of art history extended much further) and he travelled quite extensively in Muslim countries and regions: Anatolia, Syria and Iraq in the Ottoman Empire, Persia and Central Asia. During World War I, as a cavalry captain (he had been an officer in the reserve since the military education of his youth), he was sent to Anatolia and Persia, experiences he was able to use as field studies. He collected, photo-graphed, documented and initiated archaeological excavations.

The most discussed of the latter was that of Samarra, the abandoned capital of the Abbasid Caliphate of the 890s. The excavation was led by Sarre's friend Ernst Herzfeld. After the Nazis seized power in Germany, Herzfeld, a Jew, was unable to return, to Sarre's great dismay. Sarre was a conservative patriot of a dying breed, but he had no sympathy for Nazism.

He met Carl Humann during one of his very first journeys. With the help of financing from the Prussian state, Humann was responsible for excavating Pergamon (Bergama in Turkish) in northwestern Turkey. The most remarkable finding there was the so-called Pergamon altar, later brought to Berlin to become one of the main attractions at the Museuminsel. For health reasons, Humann lived in Smyrna, present-day Izmir. In 1900 Sarre married Humann's daughter Maria, an educated, intelligent and socially savvy woman. The period and class she lived in did not allow her to convert these qualities into a career of her own, but indirectly she seems to have played a significant role in orientalism in Germany. Friedrich Sarre has been described as a shy and reserved person, not at all inclined to relaxed social settings. Nevertheless, his activities were dependent on social networks in both Germany and the Orient. His wife, Maria Sarre, in a classic bourgeois manner, managed this task with ease. She mediated and cultivated contacts with significant people in the Ottoman administration and she made the family villa in Berlin a hub for the city's bourgeois intellectual elite.

In addition to Sarre's ongoing collecting of objects – which occurred among art dealers in Paris and other European metropolises – he also dedicated himself to the study of Islamic art and separating it from ethnography and archaeological research. Thus, says Stefan Weber, the current head of the Museum für Islamishe Kunst, he paved the way for Islamic art activity to be integrated into international art history. He also contributed to an increased knowledge of the context in time and space between the different cultures of the Islamic world.

2.3 Personal Relations

Islamic objects were collected and brought to European museums in European metropolises to be arranged and studied there. The peripheral locations were forced to relinquish their objects and artefacts to European cities. This was, of course, the reflection of a larger picture, namely that of the imperialist world order which had established itself as possessing and retaining ever more power.[1] An uneven balance of power between the centre and the periphery was crucial to this world order.

This is the broader context in which the museum's early collection activities were undertaken. But the relationship between these activities and imperialism was far more complex and detailed. The act of collecting and the world order were interconnected even down to the level of individuals and personal relations.

Robert Murdoch Smith, vested in the British capital interests, took what he wanted from Persia, and brought it to Britain. He had come to Persia for a special reason. He was in the country as head of the Persian part of the 'Indo-European Telegraph Department'. This was a part of the British colonial government in India (Encyclopædia Iranica). The incentive for its foundation was the Sepoy Mutiny which took place in India 1857–8. Because of bad communications, Britain was close to losing its colony before London found

---

[1] The reason we choose the word 'imperialism' instead of 'colonialism' is that Europe's dominance over the Muslim countries, especially during this time, was mainly not exercised through territorial control and settlements but with political and, above all, economic resources.

out what was happening. At the same time, it was determined that telegraphic relations in India had a decisive impact when the British had successfully put an end to the uprising. Among other things, this led the British to build telegraph lines through Persia to secure and improve communications between Britain and India. Thus, the fact that Murdoch Smith came to Persia and was able to sell carpets and other objects to the Victoria and Albert Museum was an effect of Britain's defence of its empire and a suppression of resistance.

Frederic Leighton was involved in several fields aside from art. One of these was the military. He was the head and colonel of The Artists Rifles, a regiment in the British army reserve, which was made up of volunteer artists, musicians, architects and other artistically inclined people. The first time it was really tested, after Leighton's death, was in the second Boer War, 1899–1902, as a tool in the British Empire's service.

Leighton had help from several of his friends when collecting objects in Islamic countries. One of these was Richard Burton, whose life was largely shaped by the British Empire. He was often highly critical of British colonial politics, and many of his actions and standpoints seemed – more or less consciously – to be a pure, and often crude, provocation to the decency of Victorian culture.

Nonetheless, he was captain in the army of the British East India Company, most likely a British spy, participated episodically in the Crimean War, functioned as an explorer, visited Mecca disguised as a pilgrim and wrote a book about it, and translated *Arabian Nights* into English without hiding the erotic passages of the tales (which was then the accepted norm). During the period, he was also a British consul in Damascus.

Friedrich Sarre was, as mentioned, stationed in the Ottoman Empire as an officer during World War I. But his other work there was also conditioned by imperialist structures (Fuhrman 2015). Through his wife Maria and her father, he received the contacts required for his activities in Ottoman territory. Two brothers high up in the Ottoman administration were particularly important: Osman Hamdi Bey and Halil Edhem Bey, sons of Ibrahim Edhem, the grand vizier. Both were educated in Europe and belonged to the European-influenced Ottoman elite. Osman Hamdi spoke European languages, painted oriental motifs in oil, led the academy for the fine arts and was the national conservator and director of the Ottoman Archaeological Museum. Halil Edhem, who spoke and wrote German fluently, succeeded his brother as the director after his death.

Osman Hamdi initiated and implemented a new law in 1887, which in principle prohibited the export of burial findings from the Ottoman Empire. Therefore, he has been posthumously proclaimed as, in the words of Malte Fuhrman (2015: 50), 'a champion against the semi-colonial plunder of the

Ottoman Empire'. But Fuhrman writes that a closer investigation shows that he was in no way hostile to foreign excavators. He maintained friendly relations with them and could issue special permits for his friends to export antiques. Halil Edhem was Sarre's most important contact person. Despite their good relationship, in 1910 he decided to stop making exceptions to Sarre's transportation of ancient objects to Germany. In a letter, Halil Edhem complained that 'We are treated as if we were living in an occupied country.'

On the one hand, their positions of power and cultural and social ties to Europe meant that they supported the flow of ancient objects to European museums, markets and collections. On the other hand, loyalty to their background, feelings of patriotism and, perhaps, dawning Ottoman or Turkish nationalism made them protest against the very thing they endorsed.

Thus, Islamic objects were procured in order to stimulate industrial design or to complement the classification systems of cultural and art history. But there was no particularly pronounced interest from the side of museums for the religion of Islam, for Muslims or for the historical or contemporary social and cultural contexts of which the objects were a part. This all existed in an imperial order where the centre took what it wanted from the periphery.

The social circumstances, the collection practices and the set of values of the major collectors of Islamic art are of course quite similar to the collectors of Greek and Roman art that often were procured from the same imperial situations (Lundén 2016).

Today, collections that are created in this way are to be used to 'serve society and its development'; inter alia, to promote cultural diversity and understanding and to address cross-cultural issues. Is this possible? That is what we investigate in Section 3.

3 Islamic Art

In Section 1, we borrowed two definitions from the OED: the definition of Islam – 'the religious system established through the prophet Muhammad; the Muslim religion; the Muslim of the Muslim world' – and that of religion – 'belief in or acknowledgement of some superhuman power or powers (esp. a god or gods) which is typically manifested in obedience, reverence, and worship; such a belief as part of a system defining a code of living, esp. as a means of achieving spiritual or material improvement'. Is this what the exhibitions centred on Islam bring knowledge and insights about?

The answer is: only in part and in a very superficial sense. Based on Section 2, this is perhaps not surprising. Islamic artefacts were not collected primarily for the sake of depicting Islam, but to illustrate cultural evolution and to inspire domestic crafts. At the same time, museums are framed as important promoters of intercultural dialogue in our society. Through their exhibitions they can make today's Islam accessible and understandable to visitors. This ideal of social service highlights the discrepancy between the museums' Islamic collections and the contemporary interest in Islam. This makes the call on museums to counter Islamophobia problematic, and the exhibition producers are of course aware of this.

This can be seen in attempts to exchange the Islamic in Islamic art by putting other concepts next to it. The exhibitions at the Ashmolean Museum and the Victoria and Albert Museum have been classified as 'Islamic Middle East'. This allows leeway to include things other than Islam, for example things that better harmonise with the earlier collection strategies. In a similar way, the museums sometimes distance themselves from the religious meaning of 'Islam' when they try to summarise what is displayed in the exhibitions. Thus, the British Museum says: 'The term "Islamic" is used in this gallery to define the culture of peoples living in countries where the dominant religion is Islam.' Meanwhile, the Museum für Islamische Kunst says: 'The concept ISLAMIC ART does not refer directly to religious art as such, but to the art and architecture of the cultural region moulded by Islam in the broadest sense of the term.'

What, then, is communicated when the frames are widened so significantly? That is what we discuss in subsection 3.1. The focus will be on the British Museum galleries closed in 2017. The other three exhibitions will be discussed when they deviate from the basic pattern found there.

3.1 Islam Is Introduced

The British Museum has since our visits opened a new exhibition devoted to Islamic art. What follows is thus a historical presentation. The new exhibition is housed in two rather impressive rooms which connect directly to the mostly chronological path that the majority of visitors logically follow. That was not the case with the exhibition's predecessor. It was rather secluded and the room was scaled off in a way that is characteristic of the 'white cube', an ideal for art exhibitions which became fashionable in the early twentieth century.

The room comprised 400 square metres, thematically separated into three components: a general introductory part, a second chronology which followed Islamic history along a Western and an Eastern track and a third reserved for temporary exhibitions. During our visits all of the temporary exhibitions, with one exception, were about contemporary relationships between Islam and artistic expressions.

In the introductory section, several different aims with the exhibition were presented. There was an attempt to indicate to the visitor what was on display in the exhibition. According to the first panel, there were objects shown dating from 700 AD (or 80 H(ijra)) up to the present, and they were said to 'reveal the breadth and richness of Islamic culture from Spain to China'. The exhibition thus spanned 1,300 years and countless square kilometres within its 400 square metres. This was despite the fact that large 'Islamic' East and South East Asian, European, West and East African territories were not represented. The difficult decisions on what to include and not from the vast collections of the British Museum were, as is almost always the case in museums, not explicitly addressed.

In the introductory section there was also a panel with an introduction to the Islamic faith and art in the early Islamic era. Furthermore, the exhibits in this section highlighted calligraphy, science and cross-cultural relationships that extended beyond the Middle East. In another short panel text, Islamic art was said to include both forms related to religion and objects intended for everyday use (a formulation which suggests that religion and everyday life are two separate entities). It was said that Islamic art shows a rich variety in time and space, but that there are some phenomena which are nevertheless unifying: the Arab script, the predilection for arabesques and geometrical ornamentation and the relative absence of fully or partially depicted human beings.

Whether or not the Islamic *faith* was actually introduced in the exhibition labels is debatable. The text panels did not really address anything connected to the OED definition of religion, such as spiritual content, the experience of a super-sensual reality, the difficulties people might face when trying to live in accordance with their beliefs, and the relationship between the existential questions people have and the answers Islam might offer.

However, the basic elements of the Islamic history of the emergence of Islam and its external manifestations are conveyed: the angel Gabriel revealed Islam to the Prophet Muhammad in the early seventh century; the Quran is the holy book of Islam; Islam means 'submission' in Arabic and rests on five pillars: the creed – shahada ('there is no god but Allah, and Muhammad is the messenger of Allah'), the prayers – salat, fasting during the month of Ramadan – sawm, pilgrimage – hajj, and alms – zakat; three places are considered holy: Mecca, Medina and Jerusalem; the term 'Sunni' comes from *sunna* – that is, the customs and traditions derived from the Prophet's actions and statements – and denotes the Muslims who do not believe that Muhammad appointed his own successor; 'Shia' means party with 'Ali' implicitly and those who are called Shia Muslims believe that the Prophet's cousin and son-in-law Ali was his rightful successor. The visitor also learned a little about what the first mosque in

Medina looked like, that Muslims turn to Mecca when they pray and that the direction in the mosques is characterised by a niche called mihrab. Near it there is a 'minbar', a 'pulpit chair'. On Friday, 'the holiest day of the week', prayer is held under the leadership of an imam. The muezzin calls for prayer from a minaret.

This is the same basic and reified narrative of Islam found in basic encyclopaedias or school textbooks. It is thus the exact same information accessible to most potential visitors, and the few bits of information one might expect people to have met before. What function this serves for the appreciation of the exhibition is difficult to understand.

Another of the introductory panels spoke about Islam's first two centuries. After the Prophet's death, his successors carried out successful military expeditions. They conquered today's Iraq and Iran from the Persian Sasanian Empire and Syria, Palestine and Egypt from the Byzantines. Later, the Muslim armies reached Central Asia and Spain, but their expansion was halted by the Franks at Poitiers (a statement of something fatal, and, at the same time, Eurocentric: in the Arabic sources, Poitiers is not mentioned, for the reason that the Arab attention at the time was directed East and not towards Europe (Lewis 1982). The first major Muslim dynasty was the Umayyad (661–750), whose capital was Damascus. It monitored a grand building activity that resulted in, among other things, the Dome of the Rock in Jerusalem and the Great Mosque of Damascus. The Umayyads were overthrown in 750 by the Abbasids (750–1258).

In the introductory section there was also a panel providing information about the Quran: that it consists of 114 suras and that it was revealed to Muhammad through the Archangel Gabriel. It was finally edited into a book by Uthman, the third rightly guided caliph.

The superficial nature of the panel texts vexes the academic reader. Gallery panels must of course convey brief and concise information. But it must be noted that a choice has been made here. No attempt has been made to mirror Islam as embodied spirituality. As said, the focus is instead on the most basic textbook information. Muslims conquered major territories in the 600s and 700s. Islam rests on five pillars and its holy book is called the Quran. But what about this inspires people to be or become Muslims? It was hard for a visitor to understand this. But if you visited this room in order to achieve intercultural understanding, that is what you would have wanted. If you were not a Muslim yourself, you might have been left wondering what it is that differentiates and unites those who are Muslims with and from those who are not. Is it that their lives rest on five religiously motivated pillars? Or that they can relate to this particular story of conquests?

In the book *Exhibit Labels* Beverly Serrell argues that an exhibition needs a big idea in order to be successful, communicate well and get its message across:

> interpretative labels will be easier to write and will make more sense overall to visitors if the exhibition has a single focus that unifies all its parts. Good labels are guided by a strong, cohesive exhibition plan — a theme, story, or communication goal — that sets the tone and limits the content. (Serrell 1996: 1)

According to Serrell, exhibitions that lack a unifying idea most often become vague, cluttered and confusing to visitors. The prime task of an exhibition introduction is to make sure that the visitors understand what the main idea of the exhibition is. Ideally the introduction establishes a frame for the exhibition in the form of a main statement that all the successive exhibition parts respond to.

Exhibitions of Islamic art do not adhere to Serrell's advice (Grinell 2020). It might be argued that the British Museum exhibition, like most other Islamic art exhibitions, was primarily an exhibition of objects. But even when the analysis was broadened to include the objects and their relationship to the panels, it was impossible to find any coherent message with the exhibition. Instead of an idea-driven exhibition, this was more of a classical presentation of the aesthetical and historical highlights of the collections. But even if the displays were not framed by a big idea, they were still arranged according to some ideas about chronological and typological principles.

Accompanying the panels in the introductory section was a vitrine with an unbound Quran with a carrying case from West Africa, 1850–1950; the text of a sura, carved in wood and used for teaching purposes, from West Africa, nineteenth century; a limestone capital from the 1100s could also be found; objects cast according to the technique called 'lost wax', in French *cire perdue*, whose process was explained in some detail in an illustrated panel; there were also items related to Arabic calligraphy; a few gravestones with carved Quran verses; and an instrument used for astronomical observations and time measurement, placed in a showcase that illustrated 'Islamic science' and whose text panel relayed that the five daily prayers directed to Mecca demanded knowledge of time and directions. Foremost of these astronomical instruments was the astrolabe, the joined brass discs used to determine the positions of the celestial bodies and to calculate the time by means of these. On our visits to museums in England and Germany, we encountered numerous such astrolabes.

In the introductory section there were also mosque lamps in ceramics; tiles; jewellery; a Fatimid textile fragment; and an Uzbek women's costume from sometime between the 1860s and 1920s.

In the successive vitrines there were many objects made of glass, ceramics and metal, showing the influences of previous and surrounding cultures visible in early Islamic handicrafts: Sasanian influences, Byzantine, Late Roman, Late Mesopotamian, Chinese, Greek (the exact differences between Greek and Byzantine forms were not explained). From these objects it became clear that living forms were sometimes reproduced, probably as an effect of the influences mentioned. Objects from the city of Samarra were particularly prominent, such as stucco and carved wooden objects. Between 836 and 892 Samarra was the capital of the Abbasid Caliphate. Earthenware showed influences from China as a result of long-distance trade relations.

Yet another vitrine was devoted to ornaments made in the technique that, by reducing burnt metal oxide, gives ceramics and glass the shimmering metal skin called 'lustre'.

As can be understood from this listing of objects and themes, it is hard to find a more precise idea than the effort to give a sampling of the varieties of objects, materials and techniques represented in Islamic art. The introductory sections' reliance on basic facts about the religion of Islam should probably be understood merely as a historic context for the objects. Intercultural understanding was added later and by other sectors of the museum. The idea that one should visit the exhibition to gain an understanding of what it means to be Muslim in contemporary Britain was formulated by other actors in the broader museum sector, mainly by advocates of the social importance of museums.

If one takes a liberal view, it was possible to find some points where Muslim religiosity was addressed – the gravestones, perhaps, with their quotations from the Quran showed that Islam plays an important part during death and burials. But in general the objects did not, with any apparent intensity, communicate with the panels on religion: no five pillars, no conquests. The vitrines were rather curated according to ideas about aesthetics and design history, which meant that they told a different story than the panels. The visitor was left to fill the gap between the two narratives as best they could.

The showcases did convey one thing, emphatically, however – that Islamic art, and the communities surrounding it, were not isolated. Islamic art was greatly influenced by extensive contacts with the surrounding world. In some respects, especially in the earliest period, this occurred to the extent that the resulting art might be labelled 'late antique' rather than 'Islamic'.

The problem with this exhibition, and the genre of Islamic art exhibitions generally, is the lack of focus. This critique can be directed also to the new exhibition in the British Museum (which we have only visited once and in a more casual manner). For a careful and informed visitor there are allusions to a wide range of interesting topics. In a positive interpretation this could be understood as conveying the complexity of Islamic history. However, the possible overarching narratives are lost in a constant opening of new directions and topics.

For example, one panel detailed how Islamic objects, forms and techniques reached Europe as a result of the Crusades. This was exemplified by a vitrine displaying lustre ware. The technique – 'one of the world's great technological achievements', as the panel said (which might have made the visitor wonder if it was possible the author of the text was exaggerating slightly) – was invented by Iraqi potters in the ninth century AD and spread to Egypt, Syria, Iran and Muslim Spain. In the sixteenth century lustre ware was produced in Italy and then again 'rediscovered' there in the 1850s. The heading of the panel read: 'Lustre: from the Islamic world to Britain', which could make one think that Britain was the ultimate goal for this development.

As in the example of lustre ware, cultural relations were generally portrayed as taking place between distinct and clearly separated cultures. Elements from 'Chinese culture' affected 'Islamic culture' which then affected 'European culture'. The starting point is essentially different and well-defined entities which occasionally exchanged particulars with each other. Cultural exchange and change weren't presented as taking place through comprehensive and continuous movements, processes or flows that people in many parts of the world all have had to relate to, and from which variations of common cultural forms have and can occur.

The panel that explained the lost wax technology was a unique attempt to explain how the items on display were created. Apart from this example, the exhibition shed little light on the production processes from which the objects result. Nor was there any significant information about the people who produced the objects. Sometimes a craftsman's name was mentioned because he (it is always a man) had carved, branded or painted his name onto the object in question.

It might be that the individual craftsmen's history is hardly ever written down, other than randomly and incompletely. But this does not mean that the exhibition could not give attention to how the objects were produced. Were they made in small workshops or in factories controlled by some central authority? What divisions of labour were in place? What social status did the craftsmen have and how did they relate to other groups? These questions could have placed the displayed objects in some sort of social and human reality with resonance to the visitors.

There was a corresponding lack of information about those who used the products, in what ways and in what contexts. Simple questions about the extent to which these were luxury items whose function was primarily to signal power and wealth, or utilities that people in general used in their everyday lives, were not given any attention.

In short: the visitor was met with highly decontextualised Islamic art objects, things severed from the social, cultural, economic and material environments to which they once belonged.

3.2 Time and Dynasties

What, then, was the organising principle of the exhibition? The vitrines and themes followed a chronological and geographical order, dividing Islamic art history into an Eastern and a Western branch. The prime vehicle to convey chronology and geographical location in the exhibition was dynastic labels. The panels and object label texts in the exhibition mentioned the following dynasties (if a generous definition of 'dynasty' is applied):

Umayyads, Abbasids, Fatimids, Seljuqs, Ayyubides, Zengids, Mamluks, Samanids, Karakhanids, Ilkhanids, Ghaznawids, Khwarazmshahs, Ismailites, Mongols, Aq Qoyunlus, Turkmens, Timurids, Safavids, Qajars, Ottomans, Zands, Moguls, Nasrids, Khaljits, Bahmanids, Saffarids, Bamdanids, Sulayhids, Almoravids, Marwanids, Idrisids, Tahirids, Aghlabids, Tulunids, Ghurids, Almohads, Brunei, Bengal and Dehli sultans, Zaydis, Kartids, Rasulids, Shavids, Saffarids, Jalayrids, Nizams, Sharifs, and Kakwayhids.

Forty-eight dynasties. A minority of them were given a slightly more detailed presentation, but most of them figured merely as index names. How many of them could an average visitor be expected to be familiar with? Perhaps a handful, at maximum, or maybe none at all. What could a visitor learn from reading the names of the dynasties? Possibly they could get a glimpse of the multitude of Muslim states and rulers in the medieval world of Islam. Why were they there?

According to C. E. Bosworth (1996: xv), Islamic studies 'remain much less well provided with such *Hilfsmittel* as chronologies of events, genealogical tables, historical atlases etc., than their colleagues in the fields of British or European history'. Maybe this explains why the exhibitions of Islamic art are more concerned with dynasties than the more well-equipped fields that can move on to more engaging topics. As Marshall Hodgson (1974: 23) has said, history concerns 'the dated and placed'. Archaeology, numismatics, philology and similar disciplines produce the dates and places for specific materials that can then be invoked in representations of the past. Museums have a double function in this work: cataloguing objects and giving them dating and placing, as well as contextualising them in exhibitions. A lack of distinction between the two sides of this double museum mission might explain the use of dynasties in

Islamic galleries (Grinell 2020). For the curators, a dynasty label is shorthand for date and place.

The dynastic categorisation also serves as an implicit pointer towards court culture, thus evoking a frame of 'taste and sophistication' rather than one of the social organisation of material resources, production and distribution (Haidar & Weisbin 2014: 52; Grinell 2020).

Further knowledge could be obtained from the object labels, but even these were relatively fragmented and scant. The basic formula was this: designation of the object, almost always based on the technique or material (for example, 'bowl of earthenware'), approximate area of manufacturing region ('Syria'), approximate date of manufacture ('about 1200–1300'), short description of the object and/or the technique with which it was made ('this bowl represents an early phase of lustre production linked to the Egyptian Fatimid lustre tradition. It is made of a fine stone-paste with a close fitting glaze') and some occasional words about the function ('this vessel may have served as a rosewater sprinkler or perfume dropper (*qumqum*)') or about features of object types from a particular region which distinguish them from their counterparts in other regions. One could find a translated rendering of the inscription in the few cases such were found on the objects. Sometimes the person who donated the item to the museum was mentioned. In total, this usually amounted to no more than fifty words. It was very difficult for anyone but an expert in Islamic art and history to connect this to what the text panels revealed about dynasties, regions, historical periods, calligraphy or Islam's five pillars. Beverly Serrell would have found it lacking.

As mentioned, the exhibition room also had a third component aiming to build a bridge between the present and the past. Upon our first visit, works of five contemporary artists from the Middle East and North Africa were displayed in this space. That exhibition was called 'Poetry and Exile'. All the exhibited artists for various reasons lived outside their countries of origin, mainly in political exile. It was also common that they had been either completely (usually) or partially (rarely) educated at art schools in Europe and the United States. Their previous exhibitions had also mainly taken place there. From the exhibited works, as far as techniques and idiomatic concerns, they were more strongly integrated with European/American modernism than with the tradition of Islamic art that framed the works in this exhibition. The elements associated with the latter were details inserted in a different, later and non-Islamic artistic tradition. In what way these works should be interpreted as Islamic remained unclear.

On our second visit, the third room hosted a new exhibition, 'From the Figurative to the Abstract'. This time the works of eight different artists were on display. The majority of the exhibited artists came from Muslim-majority countries, but not all of them. With this exception, the exhibition can be described just like the previous one.

The exhibition on display at the time of our third visit was quite different. This time the connection to our time was gone. The exhibition was called 'Courting to Contract. Love and Marriage in Iran'. The exhibited objects ranged from the fifteenth to the twentieth century: drawings, illustrated manuscripts and marriage contracts, wedding clothes and accessories – objects reflecting romantic relationships, Persian history and mythology. We found it to be both beautiful and fascinating. This may have been in part because it contained something missing from our previous visits: a clear connection to humans and their relationships, rituals and feelings. It should be noted that this did not mean that the focus on aesthetic forms was sacrificed, which was, and still is, fundamental to the British Museum's exhibition of the Islamic world.

If one excludes the odd modern works, the exhibition ended with the ends of the Ottoman Empire, the Qajar Empire and the Indian Mogul Kingdom, 1923, 1927 and 1858. These years, when the Islamic empires fell, are also milestones in the establishment of a colonial, and eventually neocolonial, world system. The exclusion of this period result in a large temporal void in the exhibition. If exhibitions of Islamic art should contribute to the understanding of today's political situation in both countries that are religiously dominated by Islam, and in the world at large, this void is very troublesome. It was in the missing colonial and early post-colonial time period, much more than in the periods the exhibition covers, that the current political situation with its migration patterns and power structures was created.

Can the cultural situation in the UK today be understood primarily through what occurred a thousand years ago, or better as a result of the sociopolitical patterns created in the previous century? Can the contemporary multicultural situation and the dynamics behind Brexit be understood through knowledge about the invasions of the Normans and the Norsemen, the battles at Hastings and Stamford Bridge, the competition between Christianity and paganism, the tensions between the Anglo-Saxon kingdoms, and the embroideries of the Bayeux Tapestry? Or should one rather understand the present UK in relation to the two world wars, the prosperity and fall of colonialism, the different forms of imperialist-capitalist dominance over the imperial periphery and its recurrent crises and mutations, popular culture, and (post-)modernist art? The question is of course rhetorical and the answer, we believe, is obvious.

It could be argued that Western artworks are even more decontextualised in museum galleries. The difference of course is that they are displayed as masterpieces in their own right, and as significant moments of an internalist history of art. Western art explains art, whereas Islamic art, like Indian or Chinese art, is exhibited as a representation of a world civilisation (Grinell 2018a).

3.3 Differences

There are few differences between the four major exhibitions of Islamic art in the UK and Germany. The Ashmolean Museum exhibition has the same basic structure as that at the British Museum. One difference, however, is that the Ashmolean Museum spends less time explaining what Islam is. The object labels are also somewhat more detailed. A tendency to show combinations of objects can also be noted. For example, tiles are shown in their original montage setting, in the form of large wall installations.

At the Victoria and Albert Museum, as well as at the British Museum, there are 'Islamic' objects in other places than in the Islamic art exhibition. At the British Museum, these objects are found mainly in the exhibition 'Europe 1800–1900', where they illustrate how Islamic forms inspired European artisans in the 'Oriental obsession'. At the Victoria and Albert Museum, with its strong focus on ceramics, a certain material and the results of some handicraft techniques are shown irrespective of their religio-cultural context. The Ashmolean Museum is similar, but intertwines its civilisational presentations with exhibitions such as 'Asian Crossroads' and 'West Meets East', where the focus is on relations and patterns of influence among different parts of the world.

Europe's imperialist dominance over the rest of the world is present, but uncritically and implicitly. T. E. Lawrence – the intelligence officer who, because of his political-military activities in the Arabian Peninsula during World War I, was called Lawrence of Arabia – was academically active at Oxford and his Arab clothing has ended up at the Ashmolean Museum as one of its celebrated highlights.

The Victoria and Albert Museum attempts to display complete aesthetic compositions. The British Museum strives to show connections, or the absence of connections, between different cultures and different aesthetic forms. To do this, it suffices with fragments, which do not necessarily have to be beautiful. A fragment does not show the completed artwork, proportions, combination of details, colouring or patterns in a thought-through totality. The fragment is therefore of lesser interest to an Arts and Crafts museum.

The objects at the Victoria and Albert Museum attract the eye and make the visitor lean in to get a closer look. These objects that are brought to the museum for their beauty and for the originality of their design can function in this way.

The panels at the Victoria and Albert Museum also convey the standard, superficial textbook information about the Islamic world, but it is more difficult to follow the historical narrative there than at the British Museum. Instead, the aesthetic narrative is clearer. The lack of strong geographical or temporal frame makes it easier to focus on the colours and forms available in the display cases. This way of approaching the exhibition in some ways frames the museum as such. The expectation is it evokes a focus on artisan crafts rather than lessons in civilisational history.

This also affects the visual rhythm. At the British Museum, it was even and repetitive. The display cases were filled with similar kinds of objects of similar sizes. The labels were also repetitive in their structuring and focus on standardised bits of information. This gave the impression of quantitative evidence in a history of cultural patterns. The most prominent organisational principles at the Victoria and Albert are form and technology, and the display cases are not as well stocked as they were at the British Museum. Often an object is presented alone in a vitrine, and illuminated to best emphasise its beauty. When there are several objects, they are arranged in patterns where sizes and colours interact in a carefully composed way.

This impression is also communicated by the exhibition's overall disposition. The exhibition focuses on four dynasties (compared to the British Museum's mention of forty-eight). At the Victoria and Albert the presentation of the chosen dynasties is not organised in a consistently chronological way. The exhibition's big idea is thus not about being historically, geographically or diachronically correct. Instead, it encourages the visitors to focus on the forms of a sample of high-quality objects produced in various historical periods. In a museum of arts and crafts the focus on the objects as aesthetic objects works better, and the arrangement of the exhibition also enhances the aesthetical qualities of the objects and gives them room in accordance with modern ideas about aesthetic appreciation.

Turning to the Museum für Islamische Kunst in Berlin, we see some interesting differences compared with the British examples. In contrast to the museums in the UK, the dramatic centre of the sequence of rooms in Berlin is a hall housing the overwhelmingly large Mshatta Façade, part of a desert palace built in the 700s in present-day Jordan. It was donated to Germany's emperor Wilhelm II in 1904 by the Ottoman Sultan Abdülhamid II. This façade also involves the second difference: the Berlin museum reflects explicitly its own history. The introductory panel in the entrance room of the exhibition is structured by questions providing subheadings for the comparably large amount of text. These are: Museum of Islamic art; Historical background; What is Islamic art?; How did the museum's collection originate?; and Important for you: Date specifications.

The introduction stresses that Islamic art is not religious art. It is instead related to Late Antiquity, and is said to prefer rich decor and place particular importance on the written word. The next section of the introductory panel states that this was the first museum of its kind in Europe, and that its collections were excavated in the Ottoman Empire. This explicit focus on the history of the formation of the collection is manifested through the attention given to founding figures like Friedrich Sarre, Ernst Herzfeld and persons who were closely related to them. The collection on display is thereby connected with Germany's dominant relationship with the Orient before the end of World War I, which is evoked in a presentation of Romantic orientalism, which was common among Sarre's bourgeois friends in Berlin. The perspective is not especially critical, but it is present.

From the introductory panel we also learn that the Islamic art collection was later divided between East and West Germany during the period from World War II to 2001. The 'Important for you' section explains why there are two dates on many labels in the exhibition, and that the Muslim calendar starts in the year 622 AD. In total, the English text of the panel is 400 words long.

In each successive exhibition room there are subsequent introductory texts on the dynasty framing the time period covered. These texts provide context for the specific objects displayed in the room. The texts give the impression that the idea of the exhibition is to convey the general political and cultural history of Islam. The first panel in the first room, on the first Islamic dynasty – the Umayyads – focuses on Late Antiquity and Byzantine influences on the early Muslim empire. In this room there is also an introductory panel to the Abbasids and their palace-city Samarra. Another introductory text is on the Shi'i Fatimid dynasty in North Africa (909–1171 AD). There are also larger panel on Sicily, and the Fatimid and Norman influences on the culture and art of that island. Furthermore, there is a similar text on the Sunni Seljuqs in Iran and Iraq (1037–1194 AD) (more on this in Grinell 2020). Even if there are fewer dynasties referenced here than in the British Museum, it is ironic that the museum's director, Stefan Weber, has argued that:

> The order of dynasties . . . reflects the structure of methodological thinking of the scholarly/curatorial field, but is by no means a useful structure with which to communicate the stories of the objects. Instead . . . this procession of dynasties does not serve as a meaningful framework for museum visitors, with the single exception of those who are already familiar with the period-ization of Islamic history. (Weber 2012: 33)

We can only wait for the new version of the museum to see how the great work Museum für Islamische Kunst has done with immigrant communities will affect the framing of the permanent exhibition.

Inside the standing exhibition there are also a number of thematic mini-exhibitions grafted onto the main narrative. One of these depicts the excavations of Samarra led by Ernst Herzfeld. In it, a huge number of objects are anchored in the functional whole which constitutes a city. This site-grounded way of presenting the objects gives a focus that is missing in the other museums: a concrete and limited context, a point in time and space that gave the objects their original meaning.

Another exhibition within the exhibition – it is a collaboration between the museum and the Freie Universität Berlin – is called 'Objects in Transfer'. This depicts connections across cultures that have given rise to similar forms and functions. A third is an interesting, but unsuccessful in terms of communication, exhibit which portrays the creation of a digital record of the cultural heritage which is likely to be lost in the Syrian Civil War.

3.4 Similarities

The most striking similarity between the different exhibitions of Islamic art is that they are all about exhibiting objects. Thus, of the human senses, only sight is used. As already mentioned, in this they are similar to the galleries on other classical world civilisations. Again, the difference is that these object-centred and aesthetical presentations have traditionally been content with displaying masterpieces to connoisseurs and others who care to visit the galleries. The discrepancy arises when these almost unaltered displays are given the task to counter Islamophobia, and to promote intercultural understanding and social cohesion.

They are also similar in that the narrative of Islamic art rests on solitary entities. If an object is combined with others, it is always with objects of the same kind – coins, tiles, mosque lamps – or approximately the same kind – such as different objects in a certain technique. Combinations of different types of things are rare and they do not point to anything beyond the object itself.

The four museums exhibit the same types of objects: tiles, lustre, mosque lamps, stucco and so on. In general, no museum displays objects that are not present in any of the other three museums. The canon and boundaries of Islamic art are rigid, and have not been challenged by the social turn of new museology.

Exhibitions of Islamic art still display objects according to collection principles established more than 100 years ago, which is why so little is said about the context of the objects, how they were used and by whom, how they were made, and their role in society. There is also little information about their relationship with Islam as a faith practice, even if the introductory texts can mislead one to think that this will be a main focus of the exhibitions. Even less is said about Islam as lived experience. Some panels attempt to address such questions, but do so in a very superficial way, and the result is rather awkward.

On issues concerning gender, class, ethnicity or power, the four museums have almost nothing at all to say. Islamic art comes through as gender neutral. In the few instances when the visitor can identify any gender, it is exclusively male. The concept of class is not identified at all, nor is the topic of social stratification, even if there are allusions to aristocratic environments. Nothing is said about ethnicity, even if the mention of dynasties and historic sultanates evokes cultural and linguistic differences.

The most prominent actors in the narratives are the many dynasties. They are the backbone of the narratives, and the objects in the exhibitions constantly refer to the dynasties. They constitute the highest rank in society, and they consist exclusively – according to the few names mentioned in the labels – of men. These elite men are united by their investment in the Muslim faith. But the dynasties also divide this Islamic community in time and space, and call forth an image of distinctive cultures, separated from each other. This type of boundary is even more pronounced when the Islamic world is set against its periphery, such as the Christian or Chinese worlds. Relationships and connections between the worlds are often mentioned, but they are always presented as separate entities with limited exchange.

The Islamic world is represented by objects from its so-called core countries in today's Middle East and North Africa. The Victoria and Albert Museum and the Ashmolean Museum have, as mentioned, separate exhibitions about Mughal India. Little is said about Islamic regions to the south and east of the core countries, or about India. This means that several of the world's countries with the largest Muslim populations – such as Indonesia and Nigeria – are not represented at all in exhibitions of Islamic art.

The Islamic world begins with the revelations of Prophet Muhammad. Islamic art has precursors in Byzantine and Sasanian cultures. Islamic art ends by the time the last ruling dynasties are defeated by European powers: the Mughals in 1858, the Ottomans in 1923 and the Qajars in 1927.

A more relevant historical background to today's Islamic world is found in the period after their collapses: with drawing of colonial borders, and in the experiences of the subsequent post-colonial nation states with their subordinate position in a neocolonial and globalised world dominated by capitalism.

The inclusion of contemporary art cannot remedy this lacuna. On the contrary, it further hides the decisive period of modernisation and even the rise of political Islam. This makes these museums ill equipped to serve their society when it comes to contemporary tensions around Islam. However, these large museums have been very successful at building a certain kind of bridge. The exhibitions are all, in whole or in part, funded by donors from Muslim countries.

4 Islam, the West and Something Else

Islam is, of course, treated in many other exhibitions besides those that deal with Islamic art. We have divided them, very roughly, into three different categories. The first are exhibitions on Islam and 'the Islamic world'. The second are exhibitions focusing on the relationship between the Islamic world and the West. The third involves exhibitions which display something else in which the Islamic world happens to play a certain role. We start with them.

4.1 Islam and Something Else

The 'Muslim civilisation' has played an important role in scientific and philosophical histories in the West. This is visible at the Museum of the History of Science in Oxford, which showcases a broad spectrum of historic scientific instruments.

The museum has a large collection of instruments that have their background in the Islamic world. Astrolabes are abundant, and most of them were manufactured in Islamic milieus between the ninth and eighteenth centuries. There are also other instruments from Muslim countries, which often share rooms with similar objects from other parts of the world.

At the Museum of the History of Science, individual cultures play no significant role and hence not much is said about Islam or 'Islamic culture'. The exhibition traces one single and unified scientific development. Contributions to this development come from different cultural milieus, but these are never described as delimited singularities. This adheres to a principle of teleological historiography, giving attention to that which contributes to a common and ongoing development and neglecting all the efforts that were superseded or out-competed.

The exhibition makes no attempt to seduce its visitors. The main goal of the museum was long centred on collecting and conserving scientific instruments for the study and training of researchers at Oxford. The exhibition we visited was a sample of a classical collection of historical scientific instruments presented in a purely internalist fashion, with little effort made to contextualise or explicate their use for non-expert visitors. Part of the genealogy of some of the important instrument categories is Islamic, and that part is displayed so that the visitor can immerse in the diachronic totality of the instrument's history. In this narrative science has no culture, even if Oxford is presented as one of its capital cities.

The Science Museum in London is more closely related to science centres than it is to history museums. It tries to attract visitors in competition with everything else in London that might be of interest to them. Those few who are especially interested in the history of science cannot make this kind of museum relevant. Instead, interactive arrangements and technical novelties are presented as entertaining and immersive ways to experience and learn. Like science centres, they are supposed to contribute to 'the public's knowledge and understanding of science, interest in science, engagement with science both in and outside of formal education and the workplace, creativity and problem solving abilities, and adoption of science-related vocations and avocations' (Falk et al. 2014: 4).

Science centres are often not members of the International Council of Museums (ICOM) and do not fully fit within ICOM's definition of a museum. Science museum studies can almost be said to be a field of its own, in close connection to science and technology studies, public understanding of science theories and science communication (Chakraborty 2017). Most science centres do not define themselves as museums and do not handle their material as formal collections; instead, they organise themselves in the Association of Science-Technology Centers. Their focus is on promoting a relationship with science through first-hand experiences and activities (Rennie & Williams 2002; Spitzer & Fraser 2020).

The Science Museum in London expresses a similar wish to establish a connection to people's daily lives, and invites them to have fun in an engaging and even physical way. The museum offers opportunities for this through 'events', 'interactive fun', 'movies and experiences' and 'simulators'.

At the same time, it also expresses itself in a more classical museum fashion: 'As the home of human ingenuity, we aim to inspire visitors with award-winning exhibitions, iconic objects and stories of incredible scientific achievement.'[2] Even if most of their displays and exhibitions are centred on contemporary science, there are still substantial historical contextualisations in their presentation of major scientific achievements. Most of the narratives are, however, content with going back some 100–250 years in time, leaving the Muslim golden age of science out of view.

The only Muslim-related objects are found in the history of astronomy exhibition, where an astrolabe and a model of the eighteenth-century astronomical observatory in Jaipur, India are found. This observatory was commissioned by the Hindu King Jai Singh II, who both fought against and ruled for the Mughal emperors. His huge observatory was built on a combination of Hindu, Ptolemaic and Muslim astronomical traditions. Despite this fascinating and multicultural history, its place in the astronomy exhibition is to serve as a step

---

[2] Science Museum, www.sciencemuseum.org.uk/about-us.

in a very brief historical prelude to the more immersive presentation of today's Astronomical Universe. The lack of historical footing means that the technical complexity that surrounds our daily lives appears as both modern without history and as an exclusively Western phenomenon.

At the Science Museum there are traces of a slightly different genealogy of the modern world – a genealogy in full view at the German science museum in Munich, the Deutsches Museum. The Deutsches Museum in Munich belongs to the second generation of science museums where industry and the practical application of science are in focus. As such, the institution combines the internalistic history of science model seen in Oxford with the aims and techniques of the late nineteenth-century industry fairs (Friedman 2010). It thus represents a mixture of a teleology of German achievements and a teleological development history of science.

Most of the exhibitions have been standing for quite some years and the museum is in the process of significant reinstallation and remaking of the permanent exhibitions. As they stand, the theme of science and technology is subdivided into specific themes such as pottery, vehicles, chemistry et al. The themes are chronologically structured, and most of them start in a Hegelian fashion with the historical roots in Egyptian or Roman civilisation; most of them then jump, in a similarly Hegelian way, on to the Renaissance and the scientific revolution. The narrative most often starts with locating an origin for the technique or science in question, in China, Mesopotamia or Egypt. Papermaking, for instance, is presented as a technical and chemical process, and exhibited in relation to printing and the tandem industrialisation of both these processes in a mainly German frame:

> The art of papermaking spread from China to Japan (610) to Arabia (751). The first European paper mills were set up in Spain in the twelfth century; and Italy began producing paper independently in the thirteenth. The first German paper mill was built outside Nuremberg in 1390.

Not only is the Islamic phase of paper manufacture and use all but neglected, but the evidence of papermaking in Islamic Samarkand in today's Uzbekistan under Abbasid rule in 751 is hidden behind the conflating term 'Arabia'. The claim that papermaking spread to Arabia in 751 hides that it rather was the Islamic Empire that spread to papermaking, Chinese-influenced, Central Asia – something that subsequently led to the spread of the art of papermaking into Persian and Arabic areas (Bloom 2001: 42–45).

That the 'European' paper mills in twelfth-century Spain were located in the Islamic cities of Toledo and Xàtiva is hidden behind the vague label 'Spain' rather than the contemporary al-Andalus or the more geographically neutral

Iberian peninsula (Bloom 2001: 87–89). This also makes the label 'European' vague. The label text's sequence of Spain, Italy and Germany might seem to imply a cultural entity.

One of the iconic objects of Islamic science is the astrolabe. Most histories of the astrolabe give significant room to the Islamic development and use of these. In the History of Science Museum in Oxford, the majority of displayed astrolabes are Islamic. Even if it is a Greek instrument developed in Antiquity, no ancient astrolabes have survived to our times, even if we know of them, for example, from John Philoponos' sixth-century treatise. In the Deutsches Museum the astrolabe is introduced with the following text:

> The astrolabe is a combination of rotatable star map, sighting instrument for goniometry and astronomical slide rule. It was developed by Greek astronomers between 150 BC to 150 AD. In the Middle Ages Islamic scholars improved the astrolabe and introduced it to Europe.

Islamic science and technology only have the Eurocentric role of preserving and introducing what is essentially Greek learning to Europe, even if they in passing can be given credit for having improved an astronomical/astrological instrument.

The standing exhibitions in the Deutsches Museum are an almost caricatured example of what Shank and Lindberg call 'insular accounts' of the history of science:

> Earlier insular accounts are becoming untenable as new research documents the increasing number of contacts among scholars in Islamic, Byzantine, and Latin civilizations of the Middle Ages – to say nothing of Mughal India and China. These interactions – whether personal, textual, or diplomatic – are introducing much complexity into the large-scale narrative of the history of science, which has often cast the history of medieval science as a monofilament line leading to the telos of modern science.
>
> (Shank & Lindberg 2013: 25)

Shank and Lindberg describe how the early insular accounts of the history of science often skipped directly from 'classical Greece to Isaac Newton'. The first step towards historicising early modern science came in the early twentieth century when the field of 'history of medieval science' began to be formed. The initial focus was almost exclusively European, but 'it has now expanded vastly beyond those limitations, chronologically and geographically. The newest growth area is the scientific enterprise in Islamic civilization, which is drawing more of the attention it richly deserves' (Shank & Lindberg 2013: 8).

The exhibitions at Berlin's Friedrichshain-Kreuzberg Museum, also known as the FHXB Museum, are not dominated by an older collection of objects. The reason for this is simple: such collections do not exist. The museum should instead serve as the historical memory of the districts of Friedrichshain and Kreuzberg (FHXB Friedrichshain-Kreuzberg Museum).

Islam is present in the narrative of Kreuzberg. The focus here is on the constructive creativity developed in the neighbourhood, without neglecting the difficulties the district has experienced. At first glance, the district seems to be fragmented and messy, a panel says, but in fact its history reflects a stubborn struggle for a lively city.

The exhibition begins in the early 1970s with a tattered Kreuzberg becoming the base for left-wing alternative movements, several of which featured a strong local commitment. An image of an active, heterogeneous and living community is evoked.

What does this have to do with Islam? Almost nothing, from one point of view. Then again, Turkish guest workers residing in Kreuzberg are relatively richly represented. These workers are portrayed as practically non-religious. They are included in the category 'Gastarbeiter', or guest workers. They are prominent in Kreuzberg, to the point that the words 'Turk' and 'guest worker' are sometimes synonymous. In Kreuzberg, guest workers have represented a significant part of the population from the 1960s onwards.

The exhibition tends to show the Turks as part of an inclusive multicultural community attempting to live a harsh but free and refractory life in Kreuzberg. The exhibition portrays a comradery and relationship among the Turks, the alternative movements and the general inhabitants of Kreuzberg.

But this image is not entirely convincing. In the vast majority of the photographs, the Turks and the Germans appear separately. The distance seems to be particularly great between the alternative movements of Germans and the Turkish working families. The former host sit-ins, rallies and protests. They don long hairstyles, go braless and, in the case of men, bare their chests when ring dancing at a street party. It is bohemian and autonomous. But there are no Turks seen in the pictures from these events.

In the narration of Kreuzberg's history there are some events where Turkish and more or less alternative Germans are seen approaching each other: Turkish hip-hop was performed at international peace concerts. Turkish artists have shown works inspired by the poet Nazim Hikmet and the *Türkischer Arbeiterchor West Berlin* performed concerts with music from the international workers' movement as well as Turkish folk and protest songs.[3] A former member of the choir has said that 'German left activists were very open and

3 It should be noted that Nazim Hikmet was a Moscow-oriented communist. Turkish in this context had little to do with Islam. At a cultural festival in the 1970s in Kreuzberg Hikmet fit right in. Whether a practising Muslim poet would have done so is less likely.

curious at the time. We had festivals together, they approached us.' Another member held the opposite view: 'We had nothing to do with Rauch-Haus [a nursing home which had been occupied and converted into a "self-governing housing collective"]. After all, we were the Turks.'

This is the context provided for a project that was run by Turkish and German social workers in the late 1970s with the ambition of realising a Turkish cultural centre, which would also include a prayer room. This initiative was met with political and administrative resistance, and the cultural centre was never realised. On the other hand, local Sunni Muslims succeeded in transforming a former potato warehouse into a mosque in the early 1980s. However, when the construction of a minaret began, a series of local protests erupted. The owner of the former potato warehouse threatened to evict the tenants, after which members of the community occupied the space. No minaret was built, but the local authorities allowed the Muslims to stay for a period of time.[4]

With the exception of some short stories by Muslims in the audio guide (some of which are about Islamophobia), this is the only thing explicitly said in the FHXB Museum about Islam.

FHXB's narrative focuses on an active and struggling local community with varying degrees of sympathy for left-wing secular ideologies. Muslims are tolerated as long as they are Turks and continue to propagate the image of a multi-ethnic local culture. The religious part of Turkish life does not fit the frame of the Kreuzberg narrative.

4.2 The Islamic World and the West

Karlsruhe Palace has housed the Badisches Landesmuseum since 1919. This museum is interesting in the context of this Element for two reasons.

The first is the exhibition 'Türkenbeute' ('Turkish booty') (Petrasch, Sänger, Zimmermann & Majer 1991). The museum has a considerable collection of war booty from the Ottoman armies taken during the 1600s and 1700s. The exhibition built to display these objects is built on war. It includes banners, armoury, scimitars, shields, daggers, rifles, bows and war horses' gaudy caparisons. Everything bears witness to the violent confrontations between the East and West. In this the exhibition is quite unique. There is next to nothing about violent historical relationships at the other museums we visited.

But the exhibition is certainly not only about this. The museum has taken the opportunity to broaden, deepen and complicate the image of the Ottomans and, in part, also of Islam. Besides the expected weaponry, one can find seized books,

---

[4] Today, in Kreuzberg, the newly built Omar ibn Al Khattab Mosque has a maximum capacity of 1,000 people.

carpets, tents and spoons. These items offer insight into Islamic calligraphy, Ottoman food traditions, textiles and tent crafts, and Ottoman artistic expression. Furthermore, the various Ottoman conquests and branches of the army provide the opportunity to convey knowledge about Ottoman societal organisation and administration, as well as the funding, organisation and recruitment related to the military.

Information not directly related to objects is also available, for example about the history of the House of Osman. The fact that the empire was based on continuous conquests allows the museum to touch upon the relative tolerance and respect that characterised the Ottomans' relationship with the laws, property, way of life and religions of its incorporated peoples. Visitors can learn about Ottoman culture at a media station.

There is also a general panel focused on Islam. Here again is the standard information about the Quran, the five pillars, etc. But in this exhibition the relevant concept of 'jihad' is also dealt with. In the West, this is often understood as a synonym for 'holy war'. However, the text explains that jihad literally means 'striving' or 'effort', and denotes any effort to follow God's way. This is taken to mean the promotion of the spread of Islam, but also the resistance of inhuman conditions such as ignorance, poverty, disease and suffering. For many Muslims, the text continues, jihad implies the personal struggle against one's own faults and weaknesses.

The exhibition does what it can to show that the Islamic world, or at least the Ottoman world, is a complex phenomenon, which cannot be easily summarised in a few short sentences. The driving forces for conquest and struggle co-exist with virtues that are presented as universally human and permeated by humility, compassion and tolerance to non-Muslim cultural contexts. The economic, social and administrative structure is not the same as that inhabited by their Western combatants, but this does not mean that it is essentially different.

Towards the end, the exhibition shifts focus from war booty to the ongoing contacts between Germany and the Ottoman Empire/Turkey. This, the narrative shows, has included German military consultancy in Turkey before and during World War I; connections between European and Ottoman military music; the Ottoman sultan's fascination with European machinery – clocks, for example, and palace construction; and the eighteenth-century European interest in Ottoman art, handicrafts, architecture, tulips and coffee.

Finally, the exhibition turns to the contemporary lives of Turks living in Germany. The issue of headscarves is given particular attention; firstly, through a series of photographic portraits that show how the scarf can be worn in a variety of ways, thus not concealing but accentuating the personality of women, and secondly through a video of interviews in which Muslim women discuss their choice to either wear or not wear the headscarf. Here, the choice to wear a headscarf does not necessarily indicate a generally conservative approach towards life, culture or society.

The fact that the exhibition does not shy away from controversial topics when delving into the East–West relationship makes it stand out. Still, it can be noted that the East–West conflict perspective more or less vanishes when the exhibition approaches the present day. Conflicts and controversies have existed, the exhibition has shown. Now they are presented as having been replaced by collaborations, cultural exchanges and a Muslim presence in Germany that has little to do with conflicts. If conflicts do exist, they can hopefully be overcome by carefully listening to what German Muslims say. Thus, this is a narrative that begins with large-scale mutual aggression, determined by structural and political factors, which then develops into something relatively harmonious, which can be improved by individual responsiveness and the desire to learn more about each other. This is a hopeful, albeit not very convincing version of history. Today, global structures give rise to aggression and violence that can hardly be cured by intercultural sensitivity.

The second reason to include the Badisches Landesmuseum is because of their exhibition, 'WorldCulture' (Mostafawy 2014). This exhibition draws upon the more than 3,700 objects from the Middle East, the Far East and North Africa of which the museum has come into possession since the beginning of the twentieth century. When these objects should be exhibited, the museum wanted to do something innovative and unusual: to show that history is moving forward while simultaneously repeating itself. The WorldCulture exhibition wants to show that no culture, ultimately, has been left unaffected by the global circulation of people, things, signs or information.

In order to communicate this, the objects are grouped together based on similarities, regardless of where in the world they originate. This means that Islam is not treated as a separate subject, but as one of the intertwined world-cultural expressions. However, we continue – disloyal to the exhibition's main goal – to maintain our focus on the Islamic world.

As we have seen, the British Museum and the Victoria and Albert Museum narrate changes and developments within a certain craft technique. In WorldCulture the techniques employed are not given much importance. Instead, the exhibition focuses on the influences as such. It is an exhibition where relationships and influences are more important than canonical criteria of quality or significance. The exhibition's attention is devoted to objects and forms from popular culture or kitsch; some could even be described as vulgar or ugly. One series of representations show how the Pietá motif (a mourning Mary holding her dead son Jesus) migrated from Catholic art to Shiite imagery –

where the same imagery is used to depict Zainab mourning her child, innocently killed at the Battle of Kerbela in 680 AD. Zainab was Hussein's wife and thus the daughter-in-law of Ali, the Prophet's son-in-law and a central figure in Shia Islam. From this image, the exhibition moves on to Iranian war propaganda from the Iran–Iraq War of 1980–8. It is also shown how Western beauty standards inspire plastic surgery of Iranian noses and Japanese eyes. The exhibition also shows a modest Muslim version of a Barbie doll, named Razanne.

Most of the examples in the exhibition highlight influences that flow from the West to the rest, and the exhibition explicitly aims to explain and deconstruct the worldview of orientalism and colonialism. There is also a text giving a brief history of globalisation. Even if global power relations are addressed, the emphasis is on the fundamental similarities between the regions and religions of the world.

The content of WorldCulture, when compared to the museums we have discussed so far, is original. It aims to critically discuss the conflictual world we live in and the processes that have created it. This attention is on the areas that intersect and produce similarities, where the older museum tradition focused on borders and differences. It is also original in its mixing of high art and ethnographic objects with contemporary consumer goods, something that also challenges the museological framings of Western art.

A similar aim could be found in the exhibition 'Kulturkontakte. Leben in Europa' at the Museen Dahlem in Berlin. While the two German exhibitions were similar, WorldCulture triumphs in getting the objects in its collection to offer commentary on urgent contemporary themes. This also applies when it comes to Islam. In Dahlem there was often a gap between the objects on display and the point that the exhibition tried to make in the texts. The connections between the collections and what the museum wanted to say in the exhibition were often strained and superficial. Again, this shows how much collections manage what museums are able to do.

4.3 The Islamic World

The third category of exhibitions on Islam or 'the Islamic world' was also found in in Dahlem, in the Ethnologisches Museum that closed in 2016 to prepare for a move to the Humboldt Forum on Museum Island in central Berlin. One of its last exhibitions was 'Welten der Muslime' (Muslim Worlds).

An introductory text posed a number of questions that the exhibition aimed to address. Its heading read: 'How multifaceted is the Muslim world?' The sub-questions dealt extensively with the complexity, differentiation, historical processes, changeability and relationships between Islam and other traditions in countries dominated by Islam. Focus was also on the division between a female private sphere and a male public one: with a question of whether it originates from the religion Islam. These are questions that speak to our age. The exhibition wanted to confront notions of a monolithic Islam that governs people's lives and thoughts in a simple and totalitarian way.

As with many exhibitions grown from a socially pertinent topic, it can be difficult to ground it firmly in the collections at hand. As we have seen, the collections have most often been made in relation to very different questions. The oldest layers of the ethnographic collections in Berlin derive from the Königlich Preußische Kunstkammer and the eighteenth and nineteenth centuries which were brought in to the Ethnological Museum when it was founded in 1873. This is therefore at least in part older material that will be used to discuss newer issues.

To investigate and narrate the theme of gender and space, objects collected in the mountainous countryside of the Swat district of Pakistan were used. The museum holds about 500 objects from this region, most of which were brought to Germany by the art dealer and collector Jörg Drechsel between 1973 and 1982. Swat, a part of the world which has long been bound by strong traditions, has recently, although after Drechlen's collecting expeditions, been dominated by the Taliban. The thematic panels framing this collection tried to make them illustrate the contemporary critical discussion among Muslims about gender segregation. Modern, or even post-modern, debates about gender were thus juxtaposed with comparably recent objects and photographs, but from one of the most gender-segregated cultures in the world of Islam.

Another group of objects used in the exhibition was collected by Willi Rickmer Rickmers (1873–1965). At the turn of the nineteenth century, he travelled to what was then called West Turkestan and Russian Turkestan. He was motivated by an alarmism common in older anthropology and ethnology: the fear that previous forms of culture and their material expressions were about to disappear because of accelerating modernisation. It is obvious that this view of culture stands in sharp contrast to the exhibition's focus on historical processes, changeability and complexity. In the exhibition parts built around these Central Asian collections, the narrative and the exhibited objects could not really be joined into an experiential whole.

In the large and final exhibition hall the regional focus was dropped for an effort to portray Islam as something multifaceted and non-reducible to a uniform belief system. Here the disparity of the collections instead became a strength, showing objects of Islamic inspiration and use from different times, places and social strata in a boldly non-reductive way. A lengthy and comparably academic explanatory text stated that Islam is a living tradition that is better understood through local experiences than orthodox canon. Even if there are some core tenets – for example, that the Quran is the holy book of Islam – there are numerous interpretational traditions and practices. One way of trying to make sense of this is to distinguish between the orthodox Islam of the law and the mystical Islam of experience, the text stated. The ethnographic collections displayed serve well to show regional specificities that can illustrate differing interpretations and practices. Islamic mysticism was depicted through clothes and objects worn and used by dervishes. The vernacular, where Islam blends with pre-Islamic and popular beliefs, was represented by amulets, receptacles for such, Fatima's hand and suras from the Quran inscribed on different materials, all used to counter evil, bring about happiness and cure disease.

The collections chosen to tell this story were for the most part rural and a-modern; as such, they did not bring forth the importance of Islam as a religion of trade and city life, where intercultural encounters and mixtures are characteristic.

The contemporary themes discussed are difficult to connect to the objects. The former wants to tell a story different from the latter. Modern political fundamentalism had not been collected and thus did not figure in the displays, even if it was textually presented as a threat to traditional heterodoxy.

In this respect, the exhibition was similar to those about Islamic art. But there was also an important difference. 'Welten der Muslime' attempted, and succeeded, in opening a serious discussion about the worlds of Muslims unseen in any exhibition of Islamic art. This shows that a museum's collections, and the professional and scholarly traditions attached to it, frame the representation of Islam and challenge contemporary efforts towards intercultural dialogue.

Die Religionskundliche Sammlung belongs to the Philipps Universität Marburg. The collection was established in 1927 by the father of the phenomenology of religion, Rudolf Otto, whose work *Das Heilige* (1917) had a major impact on international theological and philosophical discussions. Otto claimed that there was a mutual experience of the holy at the bottom of all religions. Rather than God, the Holy was at the heart of religious experience.

The collection is unique. The religious objects were collected for use in education on religion experiences. The objects Otto acquired through his travels and contacts were later supplemented with the purchase and gifts. In recent years the collection has also been the basis for small-scale exhibitions. Our goal was to see the exhibition 'From Dervish Cap to Mecca-Cola'. The exhibition grew out of public tensions around the plans to build a mosque in Marburg. The institution wanted to contribute to this discussion.

Design-wise, the exhibition is simple and extremely low-budget. This does not, however, affect the ability to connect Islamic collections to contemporary issues. In part, this depends on Rudolf Otto's particular interest in the experiential aspect of religion, and its practical expressions, wherever and whenever it was found. In contrast to the other museums, this is a collection of spirituality rather than art or ethnography.

The exhibition presents Islamic spirituality with the help of a large number of Indonesian objects. It presents basic facts about Islam, but in a penetrating and thorough way. Academic accuracy trumps easy accessibility or word counts. The emphasis throughout the exhibition is on religious everyday practice, in the past and in the present.

Despite its low budget, the exhibition project has embarked on significant contemporary collecting based on the theme of lived religion. Half of the exhibition is devoted to the present and concentrates on the religious world of children and adolescents. Religious teaching materials, books and toys with a connection to Islam occupy a prominent place. The outward forms of the objects are global but their functions are uniquely Muslim. There is a media station that, among other things, collects expressions of Muslim youth culture in Germany, and Islam's German presence in general.

In its modest and aesthetically simple form, the exhibition conveys Islam in a way that is more complex and lively than at other museums. It is also in close contact with important ongoing discussions about the place of Islam in Marburg and Germany. Here, Islam has been allowed to expand beyond the boundaries of the past and the core Muslim countries. Islam is here and now. It expresses the attractions of Islam without down-playing the difficulties of multi-religious co-existence. The often heated debates about the Muslim presence in Germany are touched upon in the exhibition, and the media station openly and objectively presents fundamentalist Salafism without concealing the difficulties of reconciling fundamentalism with common European perceptions of how a society should be organised.

Interestingly, the team had chosen not to include any local Muslims in the exhibition process. They were afraid that this would jeopardise the academic neutrality they wanted to offer as a service to the local society. This is in breach of the second (of ten) of the principles of ICOM's Cultural Diversity Charter:

> 2. Participatory Democracy: To promote enabling and empowering frameworks for active inputs from all stakeholders, community groups, cultural institutions and official agencies through appropriate processes of consultation, negotiation and participation, ensuring the ownership of the processes as the defining element.

A different view on knowledge and academic neutrality can be found at the St Mungo Museum of Religious Life and Art in Glasgow. Their commitment to co-operation with local communities in displaying the variety of religious life in Glasgow has attracted much museological attention (Kamel 2004b; O'Neill 2006; Amal-Naguib 2015). The exhibition that has attracted most attention is the 'Gallery of Religious Life' where several religions are individually presented, partly through the eyes of local practitioners – Buddhism, Christianity, Judaism, Hinduism, Sikhism and Islam. Self-representation is at the core of all that St Mungo's does. This presents religion as something personal and alive. Despite this, the displays tend to focus on the same textbook information found elsewhere.

When we visited, there was also a temporary exhibition about angels. The imagery consisted almost exclusively of Christian renderings of angels. The restrictive attitude of Muslims to the depiction of living beings, especially divine ones, makes it difficult to exhibit material manifestations of Islamic spirituality. The exhibition strived to include the central position of angels in Islam through a text panel and a video where two Muslims recount their relationship with angels. In the video they are presented among a group of fellow Glaswegians of other beliefs who all talk about their relations to angels.

At Birmingham University, two pages of an old Quran were temporarily exhibited in 2015, after carbon-14 dating had indicated that the parchment (but not necessarily the writing) was produced in the period 568 to 645 AD, with a 95.4 per cent degree of accuracy. The dating made world news and led to the setting up of a small exhibition.

According to Muslim historiography, the Prophet Muhammad died in 632 in Medina. This makes it possible that his hand had touched the two pages in question. Some of his close companions or his wives may have held them, or one of the four caliphs that Sunni Muslims call the rightly guided. The exhibition balanced the scientific finding with this historic and religious aura.

The pages were displayed in one of the newer buildings at the university, in a round and domed hall built specifically for rehearsing and performing music. The construction was mainly for acoustic reasons, but with this particular function assigned to it the room gave an elevated and solemn atmosphere. The dim lighting helped, as did the fact that no objects other than the two pages were displayed.

They were placed in a showcase in the middle of a circle formed by screens. The screens provided detailed facts about the history of the Quranic pages, and additional information was available through a touchscreen. There was also an English translation of the suras written on the parchment. Outside the circle there were chairs at small tables for children, with paper and coloured markers.

Nothing was said about Islam's spiritual content or about the Islamic faith. In truth, the room constituted a strange, harmonious confluence of secular matter-of-factness and sacred atmosphere. It was almost as if the dry scientific tone of the panels reinforced the religious atmosphere of the exhibition. Science had shown that the parchment was most probably produced when the Prophet lived, and it could very well have been inscribed where he lived. This provided scientifically supported authenticity to the religious historiography.

Many visitors seem to have experienced this. In the hall, there was a whiteboard where visitors were invited to write down their reactions to the exhibition. Judging from the names, a majority of visitors that had taken this opportunity seemed to have been Muslims. Almost everyone expressed their gratitude for having been able to see the pages, and many expressed how they had been moved by the experience. Some wrote about their fascination in seeing a worldly language, being 'amazed' by the age of the pages and that they are so closely associated with the very first years of a dawning world religion, perhaps its very birth. This astonishment and emotional response can be characterised as being of a historical character.

Other reactions were explicitly expressed in relation to religious beliefs. There were expressions of reverence and joy in seeing such a 'pious and blessed' manuscript. There were prayers that Allah would bless those who cared for the pages. Someone offered his/her thanks for being able to come this close to Islam's early history, which s/he 'loves to be a part of'.

We decided to include London Central Mosque in Regent's Park in our material, even if it is a religious space rather than a museum. But they have an exhibition open to the public. We were joined in our visit by a group of English tourists, consisting of, it seemed, non-Muslim retirees.

We were guided by Jayde Russell, an English convert to Islam in her thirties. The exhibition took up a very small part of her presentation. The main purpose was to give the visitors a chance to learn something about mosques and Islam. Jayde Russell was very clear that we could ask her whatever we wanted.

Because it was designed to be mobile, the exhibition consists almost entirely of panels. It was created by the UK-based organisation Exhibition Islam. Part of the exhibition explains what Islam is, and provides information about its early days. In its basic approach, it is not very different from other presentations that we have encountered. But this one is lengthier. Nowhere else have we encountered such a great wealth of knowledge about Islam. But here, too, the focus is primarily on Islam as viewed from the outside, not the religious experiences.

Much is said about Islam's earliest period and Muhammad's life. All this paints a rich picture which includes depictions of Arab society before Islam, life in Mecca and Medina, and the tribal organisation of early Arab society – maps; timelines; an image of a reconstruction of the first mosque in Medina; information about conflicts and battles.

One of the text panels is entitled 'Women in Islam'. The text begins with a description of the position of women in the Islamic tradition. Men and women are depicted as being generally equal. This is contrasted with examples of women's inequality in other older cultures, even the English, until recently. When Islam distinguishes men from women, this is described as beneficial to women. Their rights are emphasised, and the divisions between genders are said to be in harmony with human nature. This is an apologetic presentation of the true religion; it is also a fairly orthodox and rigid version of Islam.

A section of the exhibition is devoted to Islam's relationship to natural science. The accounts of Islamic contributions to scientific development are relatively uncontroversial, but the exhibition's second theme is more troublesome. This part of the exhibition posits that Islam has predicted modern science. The reason given for this is simple: since God has created the universe, He also knows everything about it.

As said, our guide gave little attention to the exhibition. A large part of the visit was devoted to visitors' questions. Jayde Russell describe how she came into contact with Islam in her university years, and eventually became a believer, which made her feel safe and cared for by God. On the position of men and women in Islam Russell answered that they are equals, as is clear to all who have studied the Quran. She also stressed that her head scarf did not signify inequality between women and men.

In her answers she described Islam as a lively and diverse religion, not as black-and-white as certain Muslims and non-Muslims make it out to be. Islam is not violent, she said: 'Preaching hatred has nothing to do with Islam. Full stop! It is not about different interpretations. The haters pick out the verses and hadiths that they have use for and do not understand the contexts in which the particulars belong. Interpretations must be based on available knowledge. Preachers of hatred disregard this obvious rule.'

The visitors listened very attentively. They seemed to be reflecting on what they had seen and, we believe, comparing what Russell had said with the images of Islam they had arrived with.

It might seem merely like a punchy conclusion, but we do believe that in this meeting between Jayde Russell and the English pensioners, more intercultural understanding was created than in any of the exhibits we visited.

5 Conclusions

Our initial questions were what, where, when and who Islam is at (a selection of) European museums.

In the museum world, Islam is explicitly found in larger museums of the 'universal' kind. There it is presented as one in a series of civilisations or world cultures. Most often 'Islam' is a culture of the medieval period, playing a part in the transition of certain aspects of Greco-Roman heritage to the Renaissance when philosophy and science was delivered to the West. The Late Antique ornamental style developed in Islamic art re-entered Europe through the Arts and Crafts Movement of the nineteenth century. As has been shown, this framing of Islamic culture explains the space allotted to exhibitions of Islamic art in the British Museum in London, in the Ashmolean in Oxford and on Berlin's Museum Island. It can also be seen at the Louvre in Paris, the Art Institute in Chicago in Illinois and the Metropolitan Museum of Art and Brooklyn Museum in New York. Sometimes Islamic culture is instead presented as a self-enclosed world culture disconnected from historical developments, as at the Museum Fünf Kontinente in Munich, the Ethnographic Museum in Dahlem, Berlin and the exhibition at the London Central Mosque. In only a few instances have we found Islam inscribed in local histories: at the Baadische Landesmuseum in Karlsruhe, the FHXB Museum in Berlin and the St Mungo Museum of Religious Life and Art in Glasgow.

Islam begins with the Prophet Muhammad and ends with the fall of the Muslim empires. It is represented by objects from the Islamic heartlands. It is further presented as a set of aesthetic forms expressed in craft objects. The persons who are seen representing Islam are male and belong to the upper echelons of society. The few who are specifically named belong to powerful dynasties.

It is often said that museums since the 1970s 'have shifted their priorities from the presentation of authentic artefacts and established taxonomies to the production of experiences where design, the originality of the display and performance are central to exhibitions' (Naguib 2015: 64). This shift is much less visible in the old, national, 'encyclopaedic' or 'universal' museums, and particularly in the Islamic art exhibitions (Cuno 2011; Lundén 2016). The label Islamic art is thus fitting in that it points to the classical art exhibition paradigm that still prevails also in most art museums (Habsburg-Lothringen 2015).

Another finding from our study is that the very label 'Islam' frames the exhibitions and pulls attention away from the specific arts and handicrafts focus of the actual displays. In addition to this, the exhibitions are focused on addressing the 'problems with Islam in Europe'. Presenting these collections within the frame of 'Islam' enhances the idea that 'Islam' is the key to explaining contemporary European sociopolitical situations. Given the medieval focus of most of the exhibitions, it also supports, if unwillingly, the idea that 'Islam' is best explained by looking at the achievements of its 'golden age' (Shatanawi 2012a).

The dominant aesthetics and dynastic categorisations are rooted in the consumption of court culture, thus evoking a frame of 'taste and sophistication' rather than one of the social organisation of material resources, production and distribution (Haidar & Weisbin 2014: 52). The dominant museological framing of Islam does not point to gender or class relations, or to other social dynamics that might be of equal historical importance. Addressing such issues would have made the exhibitions more likely to fulfil the museum's service to society as stated in ICOM's definition. Whether this means that the exhibitions or the social mission should be reinterpreted we leave open for discussion.

As we have seen, an exhibition cannot convey too many themes. The exhibition format is not suitable for that. Ideally an exhibition is framed so that all its components answer one main question. 'A big idea is a sentence – a statement – of what the exhibition is about. It is a statement in one sentence, with a subject, an action, and a consequence. It should not be vague or compound. It is one big idea, not four', as Beverly Serrell argues (1996: 1). The exhibitions of Islamic art lack such a coherent and structuring idea. These exhibitions show the museum's beautiful collections; they try to explain the development of handicrafts and arts; they try to explain the religion of Islam; they try to tell the history of the Muslim world; on some level they also want to spread tolerance for the Muslims who live in the cities and countries where the museums are located. Even so, the selection of objects is done according to old principles. These principles determine which artefacts are considered significant or beautiful; and they uphold a similarly old canon of material categories that should be included – ceramics, glass, metal, calligraphy, miniature painting and carpets.

As Fredrik Svanberg has argued, a collection manages a museum as much as a museum manages its collections. What kind of Islamic world is managed by the collected heritage in European museums? Svanberg's use of the concept of managing endows the frame with an even stronger sense of performativity. By treating the collection as a stable and 'natural' starting point for a museum's labelling of Islam and Islamic art, the collection is given strong agency in formulating what the overarching idea of an exhibition can and should be. As Svanberg states:

> Collection systems often structure the overall range and layout of exhibitions in the museum as experienced by the visitor. This may be especially true of

older large museums. The general categories of these collections often reflect similar divisions of curatorial departments and galleries or exhibition spaces. The curator is employed as keeper of a part of the collection that corresponds to a similar chunk of the gallery floor and, in this way, the general categories of the collection regulate the institution as a whole. (2015: 395)

As discussed in Section 2, 'Islam' is a label for a collection frame which was solidified some 100 years ago. The incongruities found in exhibitions of Islamic material culture are a result of the efforts to graft new perspectives onto this collection frame (Culler 1982).

The abstract and unified framing of Islam in most exhibitions does not dwell on the syncretic and the heterodox, or on the patriarchy and feudalism found in the production of Islamic cultural objects. There is an uninterrupted persistence of the perspective of 'the essentially Western European, para-academic climate of wealthy men and women in which works of Islamic art had been collected and studied' (Grabar 2012: 18), where 'the contextual-cultural dimensions of objects are not well communicated' (Weber 2012: 28). This is one explanation for the continued inability of museological framings of Islam to engage with contemporary perspectives of material culture and museum studies (Grinell 2018a). This might also explain the ease with which many recent museum exhibitions of Islam have operated under Saudi or Gulf funding (Grinell 2018b).

As has been touched upon, there are several similarities between the museo-logical framings of Islam and those of (Western) art. Most major art museums still work within the decontextualised, visual and internalist paradigm that treats art as an example of art rather than as an expression of socio-cultural circum-stances. As with heritage interpretation in general, most art museums, in contrast to Islamic art exhibitions, presuppose that the visitor approaches the material as a part of their own heritage, even if perhaps an elitist aspect of it. The aim is to make the visitor understand oneself (Grinell 2018a).

At least since Goethe's visit to the Dresden Art Gallery in March 1768, it has been popular to compare the museum to a holy place where one goes to venerate art (Offe 2004: 119). The ritual of the art museum visit can thus be described as stemming from a Protestant understanding of transcendence that by the German Romantics was transferred from the church to the art collection (Duncan 1995; Bräunlein 2004: 20–21; Klotz 2000). The museological framing of Western art is therefore quite different from the efforts to promote tolerance and under-standing (Grinell 2019).

In *Religious Objects in Museums* Crispin Paine (2013) argues that it is always easier for curators to turn to official religion, since trying to find out what people actually do with their faith requires new collecting and research which will also inevitably show the many different and competing calls for recognition within any faith group. This traditional reliance on reified official religions continues to focus on a perceived esoteric core of Islam. Not only does this belittle the richness, historicity and inconstancy of Islam, but it also explains why museums seldom problematise the phenomena that the concept of religion really frames.

These are probably some of the factors influencing the dominant tone of benevolence and beauty. Very seldom is the Islamic world presented as involved in problems, conflicts or persecutions – issues that demand arguments or opposition. The only exceptions are *Muslim Worlds* and *Turkish booty*. The first of these depicts a traditional, patriarchal system that is hard to reconcile with basic human rights; the latter is about war, something few people like. This does not compute with the ever-dominant medial connection between Islam and terrorism, violence, gender oppression and inequality. It seems as if the museums' implicit desire to promote tolerance and social understanding, coupled with the collections-based focus on arts and crafts, hinders them from engaging with contemporary tensions and thereby fulfilling the ICOM call to act in the service of society.

References

Ådahl, Karin & Mikael Åhlund (2000). *Islamic Art Collections: An international Survey*, London: Routledge Curzon.

Ahlsén, Maria, Johanna Berb & Kristina Berg (2005). 'Hela historien? Tjugo frågor till en utställning'. In Aronsson, Inga-Lill & Birgitta Meurling, eds., *Det bekönade museet. Genusperspektiv i museologi och museiverksamhet* (pp. 173–189), Uppsala: Uppsala University Press.

Ahmed, Shahab (2016). *What Is Islam? The Importance of Being Islamic*, Princeton, NJ: Princeton University Press.

Alaoui, Brahim (1999). 'An ongoing dialogue: The Museum of the Institute of the Arab World in Paris'. In *Museum International* (UNESCO, Paris), nr 203.

Allen, Chris (2010). *Islamophobia*, Aldershot: Ashgate.

Allievi, Stefano (2005). 'How the immigrant has become Muslim: Public debates on Islam in Europe'. In *Revue Européenne des migrations internationals*, 21:2.

Amal-Naguib, Saphinaz (2015). 'Materializing Islam and the imaginary of sacred space'. In Fuglerud, Øivind & Leon Wainright, eds., *Objects and Imagination. Perspectives on Materialization and Meaning* (pp. 64–78), New York: Berghahn Press.

Aronsson, Peter (2011). 'Explaining national museums: Exploring comparative approaches to the study of national museums'. In Knell, Simon J., ed., *National Museums: New Studies from Around the World* (pp. 29–54), London: Routledge.

Bal, Mieke (2015). 'The last frontier: Migratory culture, video, and exhibiting without voyeurism'. In Coombes, Annie E. & Ruth B. Phillips, eds., *The International Handbook of Museum Studies: Museum Transformations* (pp. 415–438), London: Wiley-Blackwell.

Bennett, Tony (1995). *The Birth of the Museum: History, Theory, Politics*, London: Routledge.

Berger, Peter (1999). *The Desecularization of the World: Resurgent Religion and World Politics*, Grand Rapids, MI: Eerdmans.

Berger, Peter (1969). *The Sacred Canopy*, Garden City, NY: Doubleday.

Blair, Sheila S. & Jonathan M. Bloom (2003). 'The mirage of Islamic art: Reflections on the study of an unwieldy field'. In *Art Bulletin* 85:1.

Bloom, Jonathan M. (2001). *Paper Before Print: The History and Impact of Paper in the Islamic World*, New Haven, CT: Yale University Press.

Bosworth, Clifford Edmund (1996). *The New Islamic Dynasties: A Chronological and Genealogical Manual*, Edinburgh: Edinburgh University Press.

Bräunlein, Peter (ed.) (2004). *Religion und Museum: Zur visuellen Repräsentation von Religion/en im öffentlichen Raum*, Bielefeld: Transcript Verlag.

Bring, Ove (2015). *Parthenonsyndromet. Kampen om kulturskatterna*, Stockholm: Atlantis.

Buggeln, Gretchen, Crispin Paine & S. Brent Plate (eds.) (2017). *Religion in Museums: Global and Multidisciplinary Perspectives* (pp. vix–xxv), London: Bloomsbury.

Butler, Judith (2009). *Frames of War: When Is Life Grievable?* London: Verso.

Chakraborty, Anwesha (2017). *Institutional Narratives and Their Role in Communication of Science and Technology: A Study of Public Science Museums and Centres in India*, unpublished diss., University of Bologna.

Claussen, Susanne (2010). *Anschaungssache Religion: zur Musealen Repräsentation Religiöser Artefakte*, Bielefeld: Transcript.

Coombes, Annie E. & Ruth B. Phillips (eds.) (2015). *The International Handbook of Museum Studies: Museum Transformations*, London: Wiley-Blackwell.

Crill, Rosemary & Tim Stanley (2006). *The Making of the Jameel Gallery of Islamic Art at the Victoria and Albert Museum*, London: Victoria and Albert Museum.

Culler, Jonathan D. (1982). *On Deconstruction: Theory and Criticism After Structuralism*, Ithaca, NY: Cornell University Press.

Cuno, James (2011).

Deltombe, Thomas (2005). *L'Islam Imaginaire: La Construction Médiatique de l'Islamophobie en France 1975–2005*, Paris: La Découverte.

Doumani, Beshara (2012). 'The power of layers or the layers of power? The social life of things as the backbone of new narratives'. In Junod, Benoit, Georges Khalil, Stefan Weber & Wolf Gerhard, eds., *Islamic Art and the Museum: Approaches to Art and Archeology of the Muslim World in the Twenty-First Century* (pp. 129–134), London: Saqi books.

Duncan, Carol (1995). *Civilizing Rituals: Inside Public Art Museums*, London/New York: Routledge.

Fakatseli, Olga & Julia Sachs (2008). *The Jameel Gallery of the Islamic Middle East: Summative Evaluation Report*, London: Victoria and Albert Museum.

Falk, John H., Mark D. Needham, Lynn D. Dierking & Lisa Prendergast (2014). *International Science Centre Impact Study: ISCIS Final Report*, Corvallis: John H. Falk Research.

Fekete, Liz (2009). *A Suitable Enemy: Racism, Migration and Islamophobia in Europe*, London: Pluto Press.

Fillmore, Charles J. (2008). 'The merging of "frames"'. In Favetti, Rema Rossini, ed., *Frames, Corpora, and Knowledge Representation* (pp. 1–12), Bologna: Bononia University Press.

Fletcher, Banister & Banister Fletcher (1896). *A History of Architecture on the Comparative Method. For the Student, Craftsman and Amateur*, London: Batsford.

Flood, Finbarr Barry (2007). 'From the Prophet to postmodernism? New world orders and the end of Islamic art'. In Mansfield,Elisabeth C., ed., *Making Art History: A Changing Discipline and Its Institutions*, (pp. 31–53), New York: Routledge.

Franke, Edith & Konstanze Runge (eds.) (2013). *Von Derwisch-Mütze bis Mekka-Cola. Vielfalt islamischer Glaubenspraxis. Begleitband zu einer Sonderausstellung der Religionskundlichen Sammlung der Philipps-Universität Marburg*, Marburg: diagonal-Verlag.

Friedman, A. J. (2010). 'The evolution of the science museum'. In *Physics Today*, 63:10, pp. 45–51.

Fuhrman, Malte (2015). 'Friedrich Sarre, der zeitengenössische "Orient" under der Erste Weltkrieg'. In Gonella, Julia & Jens Kröger, eds., *Wie die islamische Kunst nach Berlin kam. Der Sammler und Museumsdirektor Friedrich Sarre* (pp. 47–60), Berlin: Museum für Islamische Kunst.

Goffman, Erving (1974). *Frame Analysis: An Essay on the Organization of Experience*, Boston, MA: Northeastern University Press.

Golding, Vivian (2009). *Learning at the Museum Frontiers: Identity, Race and Power*, London: Routledge.

Gonella, Julia (2015). 'Einführung'. In Gonella, Julia & Jens Kröger, eds., *Wie die islamische Kunst nach Berlin kam. Der Sammler und Museumsdirektor Friedrich Sarre* (pp. 9–12), Berlin: Museum für Islamische Kunst.

Grabar, Oleg (2012). 'The role of the museum in the study and knowledge of Islamic art'. In Junod,Benoît, Georges Khalil, Stefan Weber & Gerhard Wolf, eds., *Islamic Art and the Museum: Approaches to Art and Archeology of the Muslim World in the Twenty-First Century* (pp. 17–27), London: Saqi.

Green, Todd (2015). *The Fear of Islam: An Introduction to Islamophobia in the West*, Minneapolis, MN: Fortress Press.

Greenfield, Jeanette (1996). *The Return of Cultural Treasures*, Cambridge: Cambridge University Press.

Grinell, Klas (2018a). 'Frames of Islamicate art: Representation of the cultural heritage of Islamdom'. In Nilsson, Thomas & Thorell, Kristina, eds., *Cultural Heritage Preservation: The Past, the Present and the Future* (pp. 65–84), Halmstad: Halmstad University Press.

Grinell, Klas (2018b). 'Framing Islam: At the World of Islam Festival, London 1976'. In *Journal of Muslims in Europe* 7.

Grinell, Klas (2019). 'Preliminary notes towards a soteriological analysis of museums'. *Museums and the Sacred: ICOFOM Study Series no. 47*, Paris: ICOFOM, pp. 123–138.

Grinell, Klas (2020). 'Labeling Islam: Structuring idea in Islamic galleries in Europe'. In Norton-Wright, Jenny, ed., *Curating Islamic Art Worldwide: From Malacca to Manchester* (pp. 31–44), London: Palgrave Macmillan.

Habsburg-Lothringen, Bettina (2015). 'From object to environment: The recent history of exhibitions in Germany and Austria'. In Henning,Michelle, ed., *The International Handbook of Museum Studies* (pp. 327–348), London: Wiley-Blackwell.

Hagedorn, Annette (2000). 'The development of Islamic art history in Germany in the late nineteenth and early twentieth centuries'. In Stephen Vernoit, ed., *Discovering Islamic Art: Scholars, Collectors and Collections, 1850–1950* (pp. 117–127), London and New York: I.B. Tauris Publishers.

Haidar, Navina Najat & Kendra Weisbin (2014). *Islamic Art in the Metropolitan Museum of Art: A Walking Guide*, New York: Scala Arts & Heritage Publisher.

Harrison, Rodney (2013). *Heritage: Critical Approaches*, London: Routledge.

Harvey, Graham (2013). *Food, Sex and Strangers: Understanding Religion as Everyday Life*, Durham: Acumen.

Heath, Ian (2007). *The Representation of Islam in British Museums*, Oxford: Archaeopress.

Hodgson, Marshall (1974). *The Venture of Islam: Conscience and History in a World Civilization, Vol. 1 – The Classical Age of Islam*, Chicago, IL: Chicago University Press.

Höglund, Maria (2012). 'European Union approaches to museums 1993–2010'. In Eilertsen, Lill & Arne Bugge Amundsen, eds., *Museum Policies in Europe 1990–2010: Negotiating Professional and Political Utopia* (EuNaMus Report No. 3) (pp. 157–188), Linköping: Linköping University Press.

Hooper-Greenhill, Eilean (1992). *Museums and the Shaping of Knowledge*, London: Routledge.

Junod, Benoit, Georges Khalil, Stefan Weber & Gerhard Wolf (eds.) (2012). *Islamic Art and the Museum: Approaches to Art and Archeology of the Muslim World in the Twenty-First Century*, London: Saqi books.

Kaiser, Wolfram, Stefan Krankenhagen & Kerstin Poehls (eds.) (2012). *Europa ausstellen: Das Museum als Praxisfeld der Europäisierung – Das Museum als praxisfeld der Europäisierung*, Cologne: Böhlau Verlag.

Kamel, Susan (2013). 'Representing objects from Islamicate countries in museums'. In Minucciani, Valeria, ed., *Religions and Museums in Europe: Immaterial and Material Heritage* (pp. 53–70), Torino: Umberto Allemandi & Co.

Kamel, Susan (2004). *Wege zur Vermittlung von Religionen in Berliner Museen: Black Kaaba Meets White Cube*, Wiesbaden: VS Verlag für Sozialwissenschaft.

Kamel, Susan & Christine Gerbich (eds.) (2014). *Experimentierfeld Museologie: Internationale Perspektiven auf Museum, Islam und Inklusion*, Bielefeld: Transcript Verlag.

Karp, Ivan & Steven D. Lavine (eds.) (1991). *Exhibiting Cultures: The Poetics and Politics of Museum Display*, Washington, DC and London: Smithsonian Institution Press.

Klotz, Heinrich (2000). *Geschichte der Deutschen Kunst. Bd. 3: Neuzeit und Moderne. 1750–2000*, München: C.H. Beck.

Knell, Simon et al. (2012). *Crossing Borders: Connecting European Identities in Museums and Online*, EuNaMus Report no. 2, Linköping: Linköping University Press.

Kröger, Jens (2009). *Das Berliner Museum für Islamische Kunst als Forschungsinstitution der Islamischen Kunst im 20. Jahrhundert*, Freiburg: DMG.

Kröger, Jens (2015). 'Friedrich Sarre. Kunsthistoriker, Sammler und Connaisseur'. In Gonella, Julia & Jens Kröger, eds., *Wie die islamische Kunst nach Berlin kam. Der Sammler und Museumsdirektor Friedrich Sarre* (pp. 13–46), Berlin: Museum für Islamische Kunst.

Kundnani, Arun (2015). *The Muslims Are Coming: Islamophobia, Extremism and the Domestic War on Terror*, London: Verso.

Larsson, Göran (ed.) (2012a). *Religion & Livsfrågor*, No. 1 – Special issue on Islamophobia.

Larsson, Göran (2012b). 'The fear of small numbers: Eurabia literature and censuses on religious belonging.' In *Journal of Muslims in Europe*, 1.

Larsson, Göran & Egundas Racius (2010). 'A different approach to the history of Islam and Muslims in Europe: A north-eastern angle, or the need to reconsider the research field'. In *Journal of Religion in Europe*, 3.

Larsson, Göran & Riem Spielhaus (2013). 'Narratives of inclusion and exclusions: Islam and Muslims as a subject of European studies'. In *Journal of Muslims in Europe*, 2:2.

Lewis, Bernard (1982). *The Muslim Discovery of Europe*, London: Weidenfeld and Nicolson.

Lowenthal, David (1998). *The Heritage Crusade and the Spoils of History*, Cambridge: Cambridge University Press.

Lundén, Staffan (2016). *Displaying Loot: The Benin Objects and the British Museum*, Göteborg: University of Gothenburg.

Lüpken, Anja (2011). *Religion(en) im Museum. Eine vergleichende Analyse der Religionsmuseen in St. Petersburg, Glasgow und Taipeh*, Berlin: Lit Verlag.

Lynch, Bernadette & Samuel Alberti (2010). 'Legacies of prejudice: Racism, co-production and radical trust in the museum'. In *Museum Management and Curatorship*, 25:1.

Macdonald, Sharon (ed.) (1998). *The Politics of Display: Museums, Science, Culture*, London: Routledge.

MacGregor, Neil (2004). 'In the shadow of Babylon'. In *The Guardian*, 14 June.

Minucciani, Valeria (ed.) (2013). *Religions and Museums in Europe: Immaterial and Material Heritage*, Torino: Umberto Allemandi & Co.

Moore, Niamh & Cathrine Whelan (eds.) (2007). *Heritage, Memory and the Politics of Identity: New Perspectives on the Cultural Landscape*, London: Ashgate.

Mostafawy, Schoole (ed.) (2014). *WeltKultur/Global Culture. Führer dürch die kulturgeschichtliche Abteilung*, Karlsruhe: Badisches Landesmuseum.

Moussouri, Theano & Juliette Fritsch (2004). *Jameel Gallery of Islamic Art: Front-End Evaluation Report*, London: Victoria and Albert Museum.

Naguib, Saphinaz Amal (2011a). 'Engaging with gender and diversity in museums of cultural history'. In *Arv: Nordic Yearbook of Folklore*, 67, pp. 111–128.

Naguib, Saphinaz Amal (2011b). 'Introduction: Patterns of cultural valuation – Priorities and aesthetics in exhibitions of identity in museums'. In *Arv: Nordic Yearbook of Folklore*, 67, pp. 9–12.

Naguib, Saphinaz Amal (2015). 'Materializing Islam and the imaginary of sacred space'. In Fuglerud, Oivind & Leon Wainright, eds., *Objects and Imagination: Perspectives on Materialization and Meaning* (pp. 64–77), New York: Berghahn Press.

Naguib, Saphinaz Amal (2013). 'Museums, diasporas and the sustainability of intangible cultural heritage'. In *Sustainability*, 5:5.

Necipoğlu, Gülru (2013). 'Reflections on thirty years of *Muqarnas*'. *Muqarnas*, 30.

Necipoğlu, Gülru (2012). 'The concept of Islamic art: Inherited discourses and new approaches'. In *Journal of Art Historiography*, 6.

Nightingale, Eithne (2006). 'Dancing around the collections: Developing individuals and audiences'. In Lang, Caroline, Vicky Voollard & John Reeve, eds., *The Responsive Museum: Working with Audiences in the Twenty-First Century* (pp. 79–91), London: Ashgate.

Norton-Wright, Jenny (ed.) (2020). *Curating Islamic Art Worldwide: From Malacca to Manchester*, London: Palgrave Macmillan.

Offe, Sabine (2004). 'Museen. Tempel. Opfer.' In Bräunlein, Peter, ed., *Religion und Museum: Zur visuellen Repräsentation von Religion/en im öffentlichen Raum* (pp. 119–138). Bielefeld: Transcript Verlag.

O'Neill, Mark (2006). 'Museums and identity in Glasgow'. In *International Journal of Heritage Studies*, 12:1.

Otto, Rudolf (1917). *Das Heilige: Über das Irrationale in der Idee des Göttlichen und sein Verhältnis zum Rationalen*, Breslau: Trewendt & Granier.

Paine, Crispin (2013). *Religious Objects in Museums: Private Lives and Public Duties*, London: Bloomsbury.

Peckham, Robert Shannan (ed.) (2003). *Rethinking Heritage: Cultures and Politics in Europe*, London: I.B. Tauris.

Peressut, Luca Basso, Francesca Lanz & Gennaro Postiglione (eds.) (2013). *European Museums in the 21st Century: Setting the Framework*, vols. 1–3, Milano: Mela Books.

Petrasch, Ernst, Reinhard Sänger, Eva Zimmermann & Hans Georg Majer (1991). *Badisches Landesmuseum Karlsruhe. Die Karlsruher Türkenbeute. Die 'Türckische Kammer' des Markgrafen Ludwig Wilhelm von Baden–Baden. Die 'Türkischen Curiositaeten' der Markgrafen von Baden–Durlach*, München: Hirmer Verlag.

Petruck, Miriam R. L. (2008). 'Framing motion in Hebrew and English', in Favetti, Rema Rossini, ed., *Frames, Corpora, and Knowledge Representation* (pp. 43–51), Bologna: Bononia University Press.

Pfluger-Schindlbeck, Ingrid (ed.) (2012). *Welten der Muslime. Für das Ethnologische Museum der Staatlichen Muzeen zu Berlin*, Berlin: Dietrich Reimer Verlag.

Rennie, Léonie J. & Gina F. Williams (2002). 'Science centers and scientific literacy: Promoting a relationship with science'. In *Science Education*, 86:5, pp. 706–726.

Said, Edward W. (1978). *Orientalism*, New York: Pantheon Books.

Sandell, Richard (2007). *Museums, Prejudice and the Reframing of Difference*, London: Routledge.

Schorch, Philipp (2013). 'Contact zones, third spaces, and the act of interpretation'. In *Museum and Society* 11:3.

Serrell, Beverly (1996). *Exhibit Labels: An Interpretative Approach*, Walnut Creek, CA: Altamira Press.

Shank, Michael H. & David C. Lindberg (2013). 'Introduction'. In Lindberg, D. & M. Shank, eds., *The Cambridge History of Science: Vol. 2 – Medieval Science* (pp. 1–26), Cambridge: Cambridge University Press.

Shatanawi, Mirjam (2012a). 'Curating against dissent'. In Flood, Christopher, Stephen Hutchings, Galina Miazhevich & Henri Nickels, eds., *Political and Cultural Representations of Muslims: Islam in the Plural* (pp. 177–192), Leiden: Brill.

Shatanawi, Mirjam (2012b). 'Engaging Islam: Working with Muslim communities in a multicultural society'. In *Curator: The Museums Journal* 55:1.

Shatanawi, Mirjam (2009). *Islam in beeld. Kunst en cultuur van moslims wereldwijd*, Amsterdam: SUN.

Sinclair, Susan (ed.) (2012). *Bibliography of Art and Architecture in the Islamic World*, Leiden: Brill.

Snow, David A. (2011). 'Frame'. In Ritzer, George & Ryan J. Michael, eds., *The Concise Encyclopedia of Sociology*, Chichester: Wiley & Blackwell.

Spielhaus, Riem (2010). 'Measuring the Muslim: About statistical obsessions, categorizations and the quantification of religion'. In *Yearbook of Muslims in Europe* (pp. 695–715), Leiden:Brill.

Spielhaus, Riem, Beate Binder & Alexa Färber (2012). 'Von der Präsenz zur Artikulation: islamisches Gemeindeleben in Hamburg und Berlin aus der Perspektive der Stadtforschung'. In *Jahrbuch StadtRegion 2012* (pp. 61–79), Schwerpunkt: Stadt und Religion.

Spitzer, William &John Fraser (2020). 'Advancing community science literacy'. In *Journal of Museum Education*, 45:1.

Stausberg, Michael & Mark Q. Gardiner (2016). 'Definition'. In Stausberg Michael & Steven Engler, eds., *The Oxford Handbook of the Study of Religion* (pp. 9–32) Oxford: Oxford University Press.

Stronge, Susan (2000). 'Collecting Mughal art at the Victoria and Albert Museum'. In Vernoit,Stephen, ed., *Discovering Islamic Art: Scholars, Collectors and Collections, 1850–1950* (pp. 85–95), London and New York: I.B. Tauris Publishers.

Sullivan, Robert (1994). 'Evaluating the ethics and consequences of museums'. In Glaser, Jane R. & Artemis A. Zenetou, eds., *Gender Perspectives: Essays on Women in Museums* (pp. 257–263), Washington, DC: Smithsonian Institution Press.

Svanberg, Fredrik (2015). 'The world as collected; Or the museum collections as situated materialities'. In Witcomb, Andrea & Kylie Message, eds., *The International Handbooks of Museum Studies: Museum Theories* (pp. 389–416), London: Wiley Blackwell.

Sweetman, John (1987). *The Oriental Obsession: Islamic Inspiration in British and American Art and Architecture 1500–1920*, Cambridge: Cambridge University Press.

Vergo, Peter (ed.) (1989). *The New Museology*, London: Reaktion Books.

Verloo, Mieke & Emanuela Lombardo (2007). 'Contested gender equality and policy variety in Europe: Introducing a critical frame analysis approach'. In Verloo, Mieke, ed., *Multiple Meanings of Gender Equality: A Critical Frame Analysis of Gender Policies in Europe* (pp. 21–46), Budapest: Central European University Press.

Vernoit, Stephen (2000). 'Islamic art and architecture: An overview of scholarship and collecting, c. 1850–c. 1950'. In Vernoit,Stephen, ed., *Discovering Islamic Art: Scholars, Collectors and Collections, 1850–1950* (pp. 1–61), London and New York: I.B. Tauris Publishers.

Ward, Rachel (2000). 'Augustus Wollaston Franks and the display of Islamic art at the British Museum'. In Vernoit,Stephen, ed., *Discovering Islamic Art: Scholars, Collectors and Collections, 1850–1950* (pp. 105–116), London and New York: I.B. Tauris Publishers.

Ward, Rachel (1997). 'Islamism, not an easy matter'. In Caygill, Marjorie & John Cherry, eds., *A.W. Franks: Nineteenth-Century Collecting and the British Museum* (pp. 272–276), London: British Museum Press.

Wearden, Jennifer (2000). 'The acquisition of Persian and Turkish carpets by the South Kensington Museum'. InVernoit, Stephen, ed., *Discovering Islamic Art: Scholars, Collectors and Collections, 1850–1950* (pp. 96–104), London and New York: I.B. Tauris Publishers.

Weber, Stefan (2012). 'A concert of things: Thoughts on objects of Islamic art in the museum context'. In Junod, Benoit, Georges Khalil, Stefan Weber & WolfGerhard, eds., *Islamic Art and the Museum: Approaches to Art and Archeology of the Muslim World in the Twenty-First Century* (pp. 28–53), London: Saqi books.

Weber, Stefan (2015). 'Vorwort'. In Gonella, Julia & Jens Kröger, *Wie die islamische Kunst nach Berlin kam. Der Sammler und Museumsdirektor Friedrich Sarre* (pp. 7–8), Berlin: Museum für Islamische Kunst.

Wilson, David M. (1997). 'Introduction: Augustus Wollaston Franks – Towards a portrait'. In Caygill, Marjorie & John Cherry, eds., *A.W. Franks: Nineteenth-Century Collecting and the British Museum* (pp. 3–4), London: British Museum Press.

Winter, Nicholas J. G. (2008). *Dangerous Frames: How Ideas about Race and Gender Shape Public Opinion*, Chicago, IL: University of Chicago Press.

Wodehouse, Katherine (2014). *The Ashmolean Museum: Crossing Cultures, Crossing Time*, Oxford: Ashmolean Museum, University of Oxford.

Yaqin, Amina & Peter Morey (2011). *Framing Muslims: Stereotyping and Representation After 9/11*, London: Harvard University Press.

Internet Resources

Badisches Landesmuseum: www.landesmuseum.de/website/Deutsch.htm.

British Museum: www.britishmuseum.org/about_us/the_museums_story/gener al_history.aasp.

EGMUS (The European Group on Museum Statistics): www.egmus.eu/nc/en/ statistics/complete_data.

Encyclopædia Iranica: www.iranicaonline.org/articles/indo-european-telegraph-department.

FHXB Friedrichshain-Kreuzberg Museum: www.fhxb-museum.de/index.php? id=1.

ICOM (International Council of Museums): http://icom.museum/the-vision /museum-definition.

ICOM Cultural Diversity Charter, 2010: http://inclusivemuseum.org/wp-content/uploads/2013/04/ICOM_Cultural_Diversity_Charter.pdf.

Index Islamicus: https://brill.com/view/db/iio.

Kulturkontakte. Leben in Europa: www.smb.museum/museen-und-einrichtungen/museen-dahlem/ausstellungen/detail.html?tx_smb_pi1% 5Bexhibition%5D=38&cHash=23f17060db6fd5094f724aa6133e3b7a.

Museum für Islamische Kunst: www.smb.museum/en/museums-and-institutions/museum-fuer-islamische-kunst/about-the-collection.html.

Religionskundliche Sammlung: www.uni-marburg.de/relsamm.

Report of the Working Group on Cross Cultural Issues of the International Council of Museums (ICOM). Presented at the 89th session of the Executive Council of ICOM on December 1997: http://archives.icom.museum/diversity.html.

Runnymede Trust: www.runnymedetrust.org/uploads/Islamophobia%20Report %202018%20FINAL.pdf.

St Mungo Museum of Religious Life and Art: www.glasgowlife.org.uk /museums/st-mungos/pages/default.aspx.

Today's Zaman: www.todayszaman.com/arts-culture_paris-louvre-museum-unveils-new-islamic-art-galleries_292939.html.

Victoria and Albert Museum: www.vam.ac.uk/content/articles/a/a-brief-history -of-the-museum.

Welten der Muslime: www.smb.museum/museen-und-einrichtungen/museen-dahlem/ausstellungen/detail.html?tx_smb_pi1%5Bexhibition%5D=35&cH ash=d25088a6b52d04441708ba0981c97eb9.

Cambridge Elements ☰

Critical Heritage Studies

Kristian Kristiansen
University of Gothenburg

Michael Rowlands
UCL

Francis Nyamnjoh
University of Cape Town

Astrid Swenson
Bath University

Shu-Li Wang
Academia Sinica

Ola Wetterberg
University of Gothenburg

About the Series

This series focuses on the recently established field of Critical Heritage Studies. Interdisciplinary in character, it brings together contributions from experts working in a range of fields, including cultural management, anthropology, archaeology, politics, and law. The series will include volumes that demonstrate the impact of contemporary theoretical discourses on heritage found throughout the world, raising awareness of the acute relevance of critically analysing and understanding the way heritage is used today to form new futures.

Cambridge Elements $\equiv$

Critical Heritage Studies

Printed in the United States
by Baker & Taylor Publisher Services